THE AUSTRALIAN
Women's . Weekly
picnics

acp
books

contents

planning a picnic

Location, location, location: that's what it's all about when it comes to organising the perfect picnic. If you can, check out the area and facilities before you set off. What you have to take will be determined by what is, or what's not, there. Most important is the availability of water and bathroom facilities, and cooking facilities if your picnic involves barbecuing. Most picnic areas are controlled by councils or national parks, so a call to them will make it easy to sort out the amenities.

the checklist

If you're going to have a perfect picnic, you need a basic checklist (see inside the front flap). After the picnic, add or subtract from the list until you have the perfect list that suits your needs. Picnics range from casually impromptu to excessively lavish and everything in between. If you're the no-fuss, no-plan type of person, then shopping for food, drink and other bits and pieces on the way to the picnic will work for you. If you're into picnic extravaganzas, then you're really going to have to be highly motivated and organised. For the in-betweens – that's most of us – there will probably be children, teenagers and a range of different aged adults, all with varying needs and expectations, but you will still need a list.

picnic basket

A fitted-out picnic basket is a beautiful thing, but it's not necessary to make your picnic a success. Don't burden yourself with excess baggage that might have to be carried a long way to the picnic. Be mindful of how many carriers you have – children may be willing enough until they get out of the car, then they are usually so excited they just want to get there.

weather

Consider the weather, particularly extremely hot, cold or windy weather, not to mention rain and thunderstorms. Check the forecast, and check to see if any fire bans are in place.

timing

Consider the time of day the picnic is being held, and prepare accordingly. However, if the weather, food, drink and company is good, the picnic could go on longer than you expect, so you might need extra or different clothing, snacks, drinks etc. A back-up of these things, left hidden in the car, can solve a crisis.

picnic rug

Rugs with waterproof backing bought from chain stores are cheap, light, efficient and washable. Ground sheets bought from camping shops, tarpaulins from chain stores or hardware shops, or large sheets of strong black plastic, bought from nurseries or hardware shops, are all good and can be covered with rugs, tablecloths, large towels or large cotton bedspreads. Drop sheets made from strong calico can be bought from paint stores; these make an excellent ground cover, especially with a ground sheet or tarp underneath, but they are a bit weighty to carry. Don't forget that it's difficult to convince children that the rug – or whatever – on the ground, actually represents a table and/or chairs, as they are inclined to walk, or worse, run, all over it; this is one issue we don't know how to resolve. Some people must have a chair (and/or a cushion) at a picnic; make sure the chairs are light, and either stackable or foldable.

tables

You have to decide if the rug on the ground is going to represent the table and chairs, or just the chairs, in which case you or some of your guests might want a proper table. If you don't use a table for eating from, a foldable table is really handy to have at a picnic anyway, even if it's only used to put the food and/or drinks on. The table should be light enough to move quickly and easily out of the rain, sun, wind, or off a pesky ants' nest. A plastic coated inexpensive tablecloth will make cleaning up easier. Have lots of paper napkins and/or paper towels, and cleaning wipes for sticky hands and faces or, take damp washcloths along, packed in sealable plastic bags.

the elements

Protect yourself and your guests from nature with a lightweight umbrella that can be moved as the sun moves to shade the picnic area, or to protect from unforseen rain. Plastic ponchos are inexpensive and are also great to have on hand in the case of a sudden downpour. Take along spare hats – at least one person will forget theirs; also take a spare towel, probably for the same person who forgot their hat. Sunscreen is vital even in the cooler months; the spray-on variety is the quickest, easiest and least messy to apply.

the rubbish

If the picnic area is already set up, there will be bins for rubbish disposal and recycling, etc. This will make life easier for the picnic organiser. If you have to remove your own rubbish, take rubbish bags and cardboard boxes for bottles, cans etc, to help you leave the picnic area clean. If you can, rinse plates and bowls etc, then wash them properly when you get home. A few tea towels and a damp sponge also will be handy.

hot or cold

It's vital food is kept at the right temperature; ensure that perishable food is kept as cool as possible to prevent the development of bacteria. Plan the home preparation of picnic food carefully, so that food is assembled or prepared as close to picnic departure time as possible. There are all sorts of equipment available to keep things cold, from small insulated carry-bags through to portable battery-operated refrigerators and enormous eskies. Freezer bricks and gel packs come in all shapes and sizes. Work out your needs for the picnic, but remember, they can be quite heavy to carry. You could freeze water or juices in plastic bottles to use instead of freezer bricks: these can be used for drinking as they melt. Flasks that keep food hot or cold are great, and come in a range of sizes; but again, they're heavy when they're full, and some are breakable; so they'll need to travel upright, just in case there's a leak.

drinks

Everything depends on how stable your picnic table is. Decide what you and your guests want to drink cold drinks from – is it plastic or glass? If it's a romantic picnic for two, fine crystal Champagne flutes would be lovely, not-so-fine plastic flutes are also available. These two extremes cover just about all types of picnics, The choice is yours; broken glass is not something you want at a picnic.

It's a bonus if you can pick up a bag of ice on the way to the picnic; make sure you have a leak-proof container in the boot of the car to hold it. Once again, it's heavy to carry. The same thing applies to hot drinks – is it plastic, china or some of those mismatched mugs we all have at home, that you want to drink tea, coffee or soup from. For children, it has to be plastic mugs or cups for both hot or cold drinks. There are many types of disposable cups available, too; these are light to carry, but they're not always good for hot drinks. And remember to dispose of them properly. Some picnic grounds have a kiosk or shop of some sort that might have boiling water available for your tea or coffee – it's always best to establish this before making your plans. Take (or buy) lots of water, it's the best hydrator of all; this is especially important if the weather is hot. Don't forget a bottle opener and, if necessary, a corkscrew. If you're serving alcoholic drinks at your picnic, check for alcohol-free-zone signs.

serving dishes

You have to decide on the expectations of your guests – also bear in mind what food is going to be served. There's nothing worse than trying to eat a steak from a bendy paper plate. Will it be disposable plates, plastic, enamel or china, etc? There are some plates available that have a hole in them for holding glasses. The containers in which the food travels to the picnic should be presentable enough to double-up for serving from; if they're not, then pack lightweight plastic or stainless steel serving bowls. You'll need tongs and/or spoons and forks for serving – there never seem to be enough of these at a picnic, so pack plenty. Pack a sharp knife or two, wrapped carefully to avoid accidents. While fingers are good implements for most picnic food, they are not practical for all picnic food. You do need cutlery; it's up to you if you use the plastic variety, those you have at home for everyday use, or the family silver for that special picnic. Pack a lightweight plastic chopping board or two; they are useful for not only chopping, or slicing bread, but also make great serving platters for cheese, pâté, dips and crackers, fruit, cold meats, etc.

condiments

Add more spice to your picnic – don't forget the salt, pepper, sauces, pickles, chutneys, relishes and lime or lemon wedges that might be needed to add to food.

dessert

Probably the best dessert to finish off with at a picnic is washed, peeled and sliced ready-to-eat fruit. For maximum flavour, buy fruit that's in season.

entertainment

Energetic people like to throw things around when they get outdoors, be it balls, frisbees, whatever so take appropriate equipment. If swimming is involved, then you need more equipment or toys, especially for the kids. Some light reading or games might amuse the more sedentary picnickers. Music can be fun to have at some picnics, but your choice of music might not necessarily be liked by neighbouring picnickers.

safety

If you're picnicking off the beaten track, make sure you've left details with reliable people of where you're going and what time you're due back. Reception for mobile phones can't be relied upon. Be aware of any hazards, such as roads, off-road vehicles, cliffs, deep or rapidly moving water, especially where children are involved. Be alert to any storm activity, especially lightning. If lighting a fire for cooking, be careful and responsible; extinguish fires completely before leaving the area. Don't forget the matches and barbecue tools. A good basic first-aid kit (see inside the back flap) is a must – leave the kit in the car if it is close-by, but if you're some distance from the car, then take it with you.

oyster shooters
posh sausage sambos
potato salad with herbed cream
apple slaw with buttermilk dressing
white chocolate and macadamia slice

ALL-AUSTRALIAN PICNICS menu one

oyster shooters

1 stalk celery (150g), trimmed
2 x 275ml cans tomato juice, chilled
1 tablespoon lemon juice
1 tablespoon worcestershire sauce
10 drops Tabasco sauce
1 cup ice cubes
8 fresh oysters

1 Cut celery into sticks long enough to use as stirrers in the shot glasses.
2 Blend or process juices, sauces and ice until smooth. Pour into flask to keep cold.
3 Divide oysters into eight shot glasses, top with tomato juice mixture; add celery sticks for stirring.

----

prep time 10 minutes **serves** 8
nutritional count per serving 0.4g total fat (0.1g saturated fat); 138kJ (33 cal); 4.2g carbohydrate; 2.5g protein; 0.7g fibre

Keep oysters well iced on the way to the picnic. The tomato juice mixture needs to be kept icy cold until you are ready to make the shooters at the picnic.

Sausages and caramelised onion can be cooked a day ahead, keep covered in the refrigerator. Assemble sandwich the morning of the picnic; wrap in plastic wrap or foil. Cut into slices at the picnic.

posh sausage sambos

8 thick lamb, rosemary and garlic sausages (680g)
1 loaf turkish bread (430g)
½ cup (140g) tomato relish
2 cups firmly packed watercress sprigs
caramelised onion
2 tablespoons olive oil
4 medium brown onions (600g), sliced thinly
1 tablespoon brown sugar
¼ cup (60ml) red wine vinegar

1　Make caramelised onion.
2　Cook sausages in heated oiled large frying pan until browned all over and cooked through. Cool then halve sausages lengthways.
3　Meanwhile, split bread lengthways; spread top with relish, spread base with caramelised onion then top with sausage halves and watercress; press bread top on firmly. Wrap sandwich in plastic wrap or foil. At the picnic, cut sandwich into eight slices.
caramelised onion　Heat oil in large frying pan; cook onion, stirring, over low heat, about 10 minutes or until soft. Add sugar and vinegar; cook, stirring, about 10 minutes or until onion is caramelised. Cool.

----

prep & cook time 45 minutes (+ cooling)　**serves** 8
nutritional count per serving　21.5g total fat (7.4g saturated fat); 1927kJ (461 cal); 38.2g carbohydrate; 27.1g protein; 3.5g fibre

perfect picnics —australian picnics

potato salad with herbed cream

1.5kg medium kipfler potatoes, scrubbed
herbed cream
½ cup (150g) mayonnaise
½ cup (120g) sour cream
¼ cup (60ml) warm water
3 teaspoons dijon mustard
¼ cup finely chopped fresh chives
½ cup coarsely chopped fresh flat-leaf parsley

1   Make herbed cream.
2   Boil, steam or microwave unpeeled potatoes until tender; drain. Cool, then slice potatoes crossways into 2cm rounds.
3   Drizzle potato with herbed cream.
herbed cream   Combine ingredients in screw-top jar; shake well.

----

prep & cook time 25 minutes (+ cooling) **serves** 8
nutritional count per serving 12.2g total fat
(4.6g saturated fat); 1074kJ (257 cal);
29g carbohydrate; 5.2g protein; 4.1g fibre

Cook the potatoes on the morning of the picnic; drizzle herbed cream over potatoes at the picnic.

apple slaw with buttermilk dressing

2 medium apples (300g), unpeeled
1 tablespoon lemon juice
4 green onions, sliced thinly
3 cups (240g) finely shredded green cabbage
1 large carrot (180g), grated coarsely
½ cup coarsely chopped fresh flat-leaf parsley
buttermilk dressing
½ cup (125ml) buttermilk
½ cup (120g) sour cream
1 tablespoon red wine vinegar

1 Make buttermilk dressing.
2 Coarsely grate apples into large bowl; stir in lemon juice. Add remaining ingredients to bowl; mix gently.
3 Drizzle slaw with buttermilk dressing.
buttermilk dressing Combine ingredients in screw-top jar; shake well.

----

prep time 15 minutes **serves** 8
nutritional count per serving 6.4g total fat
(4.1g saturated fat); 410kJ (98 cal);
7.1g carbohydrate; 1.8g protein; 2.5g fibre

We used pink lady apples and savoy cabbage. Grate the apple and mix with the juice on the morning of the picnic. Assemble and dress the slaw at the picnic.

The slice can be made up to four days ahead; store in an airtight container.

white chocolate and macadamia slice

100g unsalted butter, chopped coarsely
400g white eating chocolate, chopped coarsely
¾ cup (165g) caster sugar
4 eggs
2 cups (300g) self raising flour
1 teaspoon vanilla extract
1 cup (140g) macadamia nuts, chopped finely
2 tablespoons icing sugar

1 Preheat oven to 170°C/150°C fan-forced. Grease 22cm x 32cm lamington pan; line base and two long sides with baking paper, extending paper 5cm over sides.
2 Combine butter and chocolate in medium saucepan; stir over low heat until smooth. Remove from heat; stir in sugar. Cool 10 minutes.
3 Stir in eggs, then sifted flour, extract and nuts. Spread mixture into pan. Bake about 30 minutes. Cool in pan.
4 Turn slice, top-side up, onto board; cut into squares then dust with sifted icing sugar.

----

prep & cook time 55 minutes makes 24
nutritional count per serving 14.6g total fat
(6.7g saturated fat); 1041kJ (249 cal);
26g carbohydrate; 4.1g protein; 0.8g fibre

best-ever chicken sandwiches
prawns with garlic and gherkin mayonnaise
cos salad with basil dressing
smoked trout asparagus pasta salad
mini pavlovas with vanilla strawberries

ALL-AUSTRALIAN PICNICS menu two

best-ever chicken sandwiches

600g chicken breast fillets
½ cup (150g) mayonnaise
¼ cup coarsely chopped fresh flat leaf parsley
8 slices white sandwich bread (360g)
40g butter, softened

1   Place chicken in medium saucepan; add enough cold water to cover. Bring to the boil, reduce heat; simmer 10 minutes. Remove from heat. Stand 30 minutes; drain.

2   Cut chicken into 2cm pieces, combine in medium bowl with mayonnaise and parsley.

3   Spread each bread slice with butter. Sandwich chicken mixture between bread slices. Cut each sandwich into quarters.

----

prep & cook time 25 minutes (+ standing) **serves** 8
nutritional count per serving 15.5g total fat
(4.8g saturated fat); 1329kJ (318 cal);
23.9g carbohydrate; 20.1g protein; 1.5g fibre

The chicken mixture can be made a day before the picnic, keep refrigerated. Make the sandwiches on the morning of the picnic, wrap tightly in plastic wrap or foil. We like to keep the crusts on the bread. Use a whole-egg mayonnaise for the creamiest-tasting filling.

The prawns and the garlic and gherkin mayonnaise can be prepared a day before the picnic; keep covered in the refrigerator.

prawns with garlic and gherkin mayonnaise

24 cooked medium king prawns (1kg)
garlic and gherkin mayonnaise
2 egg yolks
3 teaspoons dijon mustard
2 tablespoons lemon juice
2 cloves garlic
pinch caster sugar
⅔ cup (160ml) light olive oil
¼ cup (45g) finely chopped baby gherkins
¼ cup coarsely chopped fresh flat-leaf parsley

1 Make garlic and gherkin mayonnaise.
2 Shell and devein prawns leaving tails intact.
3 Serve prawns with mayonnaise for dipping.
garlic and gherkin mayonnaise Blend or process egg yolks, mustard, juice, garlic and sugar. With motor operating, add oil in a thin steady stream until mayonnaise is thick. Stir in gherkins and parsley.

----

prep & cook time 15 minutes **serves** 8
nutritional count per serving 19.9g total fat (3g saturated fat); 1007kJ (241 cal); 2g carbohydrate; 13.7g protein; 0.4g fibre

Baby gherkins, also known as cornichons, are a very small variety of pickled cucumber; when pickled with dill they are known as a dill pickle. Baby gherkins are available from major supermarkets and delicatessens.

Prepare the bacon, lettuce and dressing on the morning of the picnic. Assemble the salad at the picnic. The ice cubes will "hold" the colour in the dressing.

cos salad with basil dressing

4 rindless bacon rashers (260g), sliced thinly
3 baby cos lettuce, trimmed, leaves separated
basil dressing
⅓ cup firmly packed fresh basil leaves
⅓ cup firmly packed fresh flat-leaf parsley leaves
¼ cup (60ml) white wine vinegar
¼ cup (60ml) olive oil
1 tablespoon wholegrain mustard
3 ice cubes

1 Make basil dressing; season to taste.
2 Cook bacon in heated oiled large frying pan until crisp; drain on absorbent paper.
3 Arrange lettuce leaves in large bowl, sprinkle with bacon, drizzle with dressing.
basil dressing Blend or process ingredients until smooth.

prep & cook time 15 minutes **serves** 8
nutritional count per serving 9.9g total fat (2g saturated fat); 543kJ (130 cal); 1.5g carbohydrate; 7.7g protein; 1.6g fibre

The salad is best made and assembled on the morning of the picnic. We used wood-smoked rainbow trout in this recipe.

smoked trout and asparagus pasta salad

340g asparagus, trimmed
250g penne pasta
½ cup (150g) mayonnaise
¼ cup (60ml) lemon juice
½ cup coarsely chopped fresh flat-leaf parsley
1½ tablespoons rinsed, drained baby capers
2 green onions, sliced thinly
300g smoked trout, flaked

1 Cut asparagus into 5cm lengths. Boil, steam or microwave asparagus until tender; drain. Rinse under cold water; drain.

2 Cook pasta in large saucepan of boiling water until tender; drain. Rinse under cold water; drain.

3 Combine mayonnaise and juice in large bowl; stir in parsley, capers, onion, asparagus, trout and pasta.

----

prep & cook time 25 minutes **serves** 8
nutritional count per serving 8.3g total fat
(1.2g saturated fat); 1003kJ (240 cal);
25.9g carbohydrate; 14g protein; 1.8g fibre

Pavlovas can be made a week ahead, store in an airtight container at room temperature. Prepare the strawberries on the morning of the picnic. Assemble the pavlovas at the picnic as close to serving time as possible.

mini pavlovas with vanilla strawberries

4 egg whites
1 cup (220g) caster sugar
1 tablespoon cornflour
⅔ cup (160ml) thick pure cream
vanilla strawberries
1 cup (220g) caster sugar
½ cup (125ml) water
2 teaspoons vanilla extract
500g strawberries, halved

1   Preheat oven to 120°C/100°C fan-forced. Grease two oven trays; line with baking paper. Draw 8 x 8cm rounds on baking paper.
2   Beat egg whites in small bowl with electric mixer until soft peaks form. Gradually add sugar; beat until sugar dissolves between additions. Beat in sifted cornflour.
3   Spoon meringue mixture into rounds; make hollows in meringue using back of a dessertspoon. Bake pavlovas about 1¼ hours. Cool pavlovas in oven with door ajar.
4   Make vanilla strawberries.
5   Serve pavlovas topped with cream and strawberries.
vanilla strawberries Combine sugar and the water in small saucepan. Stir over heat until sugar dissolves; bring to the boil. Boil, uncovered, without stirring, 2 minutes. Remove from heat; stir in extract. Place strawberries in medium bowl; stir in syrup. Cool.

----

prep & cook time 1 hour 30 minutes (+ cooling)
makes 8
nutritional count per pavlova 10.5g total fat (6.8g saturated fat); 1388kJ (332 cal); 58.4g carbohydrate; 3.1g protein; 1.4g fibre

The cream used here is thick pure cream (containing 66 percent fat), which doesn't need to be whipped. Just spoon it out of its container onto the pavlovas.

baked ricotta
peppered rare roast beef
baby rocket quiche
summer garden salad
berry delicious

ALL-AUSTRALIAN PICNICS menu three

baked ricotta

500g fresh ricotta cheese
2 garlic cloves, chopped finely
½ teaspoon dried chilli flakes
½ teaspoon fresh thyme leaves
2 tablespoons finely grated parmesan cheese
2 tablespoons olive oil
120g packet flatbread
90g jar tomato tapenade

1   Press ricotta into 12cm sieve; place over bowl, cover. Refrigerate 4 hours or overnight.
2   Preheat oven to 180°C/160°C fan-forced. Grease oven tray, line with baking paper.
3   Turn ricotta onto tray; sprinkle with garlic, chilli, thyme and parmesan; drizzle with oil. Bake, uncovered, about 30 minutes or until cheese is browned lightly. Cool.
4   Serve ricotta with flatbread and tomato tapenade.

----

prep & cook time 40 minutes (+ refrigeration) **serves** 8
nutritional count per serving 17g total fat
(6.5g saturated fat); 986kJ (236 cal);
10.7g carbohydrate; 10g protein; 0.9g fibre

The ricotta is best prepared and baked on the morning of the picnic.

peppered rare roast beef

1 tablespoon cracked black pepper
2 x 500g pieces trimmed beef eye fillet
1 tablespoon vegetable oil
½ cup coarsely chopped fresh flat-leaf parsley
¼ cup finely chopped fresh chives
2 tablespoons dijon mustard

1 Preheat oven to 200°C/180°C fan-forced.
2 Sprinkle pepper over a sheet of baking paper; roll beef in the pepper.
3 Heat oil in medium shallow flameproof baking dish over high heat; add beef, turn until browned all over. Transfer dish to oven; roast beef 20 minutes, turning after 10 minutes for medium-rare, or roast until cooked to your liking.

4 Remove beef from dish to plate; cover tightly with foil. Cool.
5 Spread herbs over sheet of baking paper. Brush beef with mustard; roll beef firmly in herb mixture.
6 Serve beef, sliced thinly, on crusty buttered bread rolls with watercress and a little extra dijon mustard.

----

prep & cook time 35 minutes **serves** 8
nutritional count per serving 8.4g total fat (2.9g saturated fat); 769kJ (184 cal); 0.2g carbohydrate; 26.4g protein; 0.3g fibre

Beef can be cooked a day before the picnic. Slice beef at the picnic.

Quiche can be made a day ahead, keep covered in the refrigerator. You can also make and bake the pastry case a day or two ahead, then add and bake the filling on picnic day.

baby rocket quiche

50g baby rocket leaves, chopped finely
3 eggs
1 egg yolk
¾ cup (180ml) cream
pastry
1¼ cups (185g) plain flour
125g cold butter, chopped coarsely
1 egg yolk
2 teaspoons iced water

1 Make pastry.
2 Preheat oven to 200°C/180°C fan-forced.
3 Grease shallow 20cm-round loose-based tart tin. Roll pastry out on floured surface until 4mm thick. Ease pastry into tin, press into base and side; prick base all over with fork. Cover, refrigerate 20 minutes.
4 Line pastry with baking paper; fill with dried beans or rice. Bake 12 minutes; carefully remove paper and rice. Bake about 8 minutes or until pastry is browned lightly. Reduce oven temperature to 160°C/140°C fan-forced.
5 Sprinkle rocket into pastry case. Whisk eggs, egg yolk and cream in medium jug; pour over rocket. Bake quiche about 40 minutes or until set. Cool.
pastry Process flour and butter until crumbly. Add egg yolk and the water, pulse until ingredients come together. Knead pastry on floured surface until smooth; cover; refrigerate 20 minutes.

----

prep & cook time 1 hour 20 minutes
(+ refrigeration & cooling) **serves** 8
nutritional count per serving 25.9g total fat
(15.6g saturated fat); 1375kJ (329 cal);
17.6g carbohydrate; 6.7g protein; 1g fibre

Prepare the tomato mixture, lettuce and cucumber on the morning of the picnic. Assemble the salad at the picnic.

summer garden salad

2 tablespoons red wine vinegar

¼ cup (60ml) olive oil

pinch caster sugar

4 medium tomatoes (600g), seeded, chopped finely

1 green butter lettuce, leaves separated

1 lebanese cucumber (130g), halved, seeded, sliced thinly

2 medium avocados (500g), sliced thickly crossways

1 Combine vinegar, oil, sugar and tomato in small bowl.

2 Combine lettuce, cucumber and avocado on plate; top with tomato mixture.

----

prep time 10 minutes **serves** 8

nutritional count per serving 16.8g total fat (3.1g saturated fat); 681kJ (163 cal); 1.2g carbohydrate; 1.4g protein; 1.6g fibre

Use any type or combination of berries you like. We used a combination of boysenberries, raspberries and cherries. The berries can be cooked the day before the picnic, refrigerate, covered, overnight. If you prefer, serve the berries with thick double cream or chocolate or vanilla ice-cream if it's available at your picnic destination.

berry delicious

500g frozen berries
¼ cup (55g) caster sugar
1 vanilla bean
⅔ cup (190g) greek-style yogurt

1 Combine berries and sugar in medium saucepan. Split vanilla bean, scrape seeds into berry mixture; add bean to pan. Cook over medium heat about 3 minutes, stirring occasionally, or until berries begin to soften. Cool.
2 Transfer berry mixture to container, then cover and refrigerate overnight.
3 Discard vanilla bean; serve berries with yogurt.

----

prep & cook time 10 minutes (+ refrigeration) **serves** 8
nutritional count per serving 0.7g total fat
(0.3g saturated fat); 305kJ (73 cal);
13.1g carbohydrate; 1.9g protein; 2.9g fibre

sumac labne with coppa
chickpea and walnut salad with green chilli
fennel and preserved lemon salad with haloumi
lamb with baba ghanoush and rocket
caramel apples with cinnamon yogurt

MIDDLE-EASTERN PICNICS menu one

sumac labne with coppa

3 cups (840g) greek-style yogurt
3 teaspoons fine table salt
2 tablespoons olive oil
2 teaspoons sumac
24 slices mild coppa (360g)

1   Combine yogurt and salt in medium bowl; spoon
into muslin-lined large colander or sieve placed over
bowl. Gather corners of muslin together, twist then tie
with kitchen string. Place a plate on top of the muslin,
then weight with two or three heavy cans; refrigerate
24 hours.

2   Place yogurt in medium bowl; discard muslin. Using
oiled hands, roll level tablespoons of yogurt into balls;
roll in oil then sprinkle with sumac.

3   Serve labne with coppa, and lavash crisps, if you like.

prep time 15 minutes (+ refrigeration) **serves 8**
nutritional count per serving 28.8g total fat
(11g saturated fat); 1505kJ (360 cal);
10g carbohydrate; 15.5g protein; 0g fibre

Labne can be left to drain and thicken, still weighted,
in the fridge for up to three days. Finish the labne on
the morning of the picnic.

Prepare the dressing and assemble the salad on the morning of the picnic. Dress the salad at the picnic.

chickpea and walnut salad with green chilli

¼ cup (60ml) olive oil
¼ cup (60ml) lemon juice
2 x 400g cans chickpeas, rinsed, drained
1 cup coarsely chopped fresh flat-leaf parsley
1 cup coarsely chopped fresh mint
1 cup (160g) seeded green olives, chopped coarsely
4 green onions, sliced thinly
2 long green chillies, sliced thinly
1 medium red capsicum (200g), chopped finely
1 cup (100g) roasted walnuts, chopped coarsely

1   To make dressing, place oil and juice in screw-top jar; shake well.
2   Combine remaining ingredients in large bowl; drizzle with dressing before serving.

----

prep time 20 minutes **serves** 8
nutritional count per serving 17.7g total fat
(1.8g saturated fat); 1053kJ (252 cal);
14.7g carbohydrate; 6.6g protein; 5.1g fibre

Prepare the cheese and salad on the morning of the picnic. Pan-fry the haloumi as close to departure time as possible; don't over cook it or it will toughen. It is best to use a non-stick pan for frying haloumi. Combining the avocado, oil and juice in the bowl will help stop the avocado from turning brown.

fennel and preserved lemon salad with haloumi

250g haloumi cheese, sliced thinly
1 tablespoon finely chopped fresh coriander
1 tablespoon olive oil
1 tablespoon lemon juice
fennel and preserved lemon salad
1 medium avocado (250g), chopped coarsely
1 tablespoon lemon juice
2 tablespoons olive oil
2 pieces preserved lemon rind (80g), washed, chopped finely
2 medium fennel bulbs (600g), sliced thinly
½ cup firmly packed fresh coriander leaves

1 Make fennel and preserved lemon salad.
2 Combine cheese, coriander, oil and juice in small bowl. Heat large frying pan; cook cheese over medium heat until browned both sides.
3 Serve cheese topped with salad.
fennel and preserved lemon salad Combine avocado, juice and oil in medium bowl. Add remaining ingredients; toss gently before serving.

----

prep & cook time 25 minutes **serves** 8
nutritional count per serving 17.2g total fat (5.5g saturated fat); 811kJ (194 cal); 2.1g carbohydrate; 7.5g protein; 1.5g fibre

Lamb can be prepared and refrigerated the day before, but is best cooked on the morning of the picnic. Fill the pittas as close to departure time as possible.

Baba ghanoush is a roasted eggplant (aubergine) dip or spread. It is available from delicatessens and most supermarkets.

lamb with baba ghanoush and rocket

500g lamb backstrap
1 teaspoon finely grated lemon rind
1 tablespoon za'atar
1 tablespoon olive oil
4 pocket pitta breads (260g), halved
250g baba ghanoush
50g baby rocket leaves

1 Combine lamb, rind, za'atar and oil in medium bowl.
2 Cook lamb in heated, oiled large frying pan over high heat until cooked to your liking. Cover lamb; stand 10 minutes then slice thinly.
3 Spread inside of pittas with baba ghanoush; fill with lamb and rocket.

----

prep & cook time 20 minutes **serves** 8
nutritional count per serving 7.7g total fat
2.5g saturated fat); 895kJ (214 cal);
18.6g carbohydrate; 16.5g protein; 1.8g fibre

We used pink lady apples, but any type will be fine. The apples are best cooked on the morning of the picnic.
If you prefer, crème fraîche, mascarpone or whipped cream can be flavoured and used instead of the yogurt.

caramel apples with cinnamon yogurt

8 small apples (1kg)
2 tablespoons lemon juice
3 cups (660g) caster sugar
¾ cup (180ml) water
125g unsalted butter, chopped coarsely
2 cups (560g) greek-style yogurt
1 tablespoon honey
1 teaspoon ground cinnamon
pinch ground ginger

1 Combine peeled apples and juice in medium bowl.
2 Combine sugar, the water and butter in large saucepan; stir over low heat until sugar dissolves. Bring to boil; reduce heat, simmer, without stirring about 15 minutes, shaking pan occasionally until dark caramel colour. Allow bubbles to subside.
3 Meanwhile, preheat oven to 180°C/160°C fan-forced. Grease 2.5-litre (10-cup) ovenproof dish.
4 Place apples in dish, pour caramel over apples; cover with greased foil. Bake about 30 minutes or until apples are tender. Cool.
5 Combine yogurt with honey, cinnamon and ginger in small bowl.
6 Serve apples with yogurt mixture.

----

prep & cook time 45 minutes (+ cooling) **serves** 8
nutritional count per serving 18g total fat (11.8g saturated fat); 2404kJ (575 cal); 102.6g carbohydrate; 4.3g protein, 1.7g fibre

lamb tart with eggplant and
   goats cheese
couscous salad with mixed peas
   and beans
chilli chicken skewers with coriander
baby carrot and fresh beetroot salad
ginger cakes with orange glaze

lamb tart with eggplant and goats cheese

1½ sheets ready-rolled shortcrust pastry
1 tablespoon olive oil
1 medium red capsicum (200g), chopped finely
2 teaspoons ground cumin
1 teaspoon sweet paprika
½ teaspoon ground turmeric
500g lamb mince
1 egg, beaten lightly
¼ cup finely chopped fresh coriander
¼ cup finely chopped fresh flat-leaf parsley
150g char-grilled eggplant, drained,
   chopped coarsely
60g firm goats cheese, crumbled coarsely

1   Preheat oven to 220°C/200°C fan-forced. Grease 12cm x 35cm loose-based flan tin.
2   Join pastry pieces together by rubbing one edge with a little water and pressing to seal. Ease pastry into tin; press into base and sides. Trim edge; prick base with fork. Line pastry with baking paper, fill with beans or rice. Bake 10 minutes, remove rice and paper; bake a further 10 minutes or until pastry is golden brown.
3   Meanwhile, heat oil in large frying pan; cook capsicum, spices and lamb until lamb is browned and liquid evaporated. Cool. Stir in egg and herbs.
4   Spoon lamb mixture into pastry case, top with eggplant and cheese. Bake about 12 minutes. Cool before cutting.

-----

prep & cook time 50 minutes (+ cooling) **serves** 8
nutritional count per serving 14.7g total fat (8.9g saturated fat); 1287kJ (308 cal); 15.3g carbohydrate; 17.3g protein; 1.4g fibre

The tart can be made a day before the picnic; keep covered in the fridge.

couscous salad with mixed peas and beans

1 cup (200g) couscous
2 tablespoons lemon juice
1 cup (250ml) boiling water
150g baby green beans, trimmed, halved
150g sugar snap peas, trimmed
1 cup (120g) frozen baby green peas
1½ tablespoons wholegrain mustard
¼ cup (60ml) olive oil
¼ cup finely chopped fresh chives

1 Combine couscous, juice and the water in medium heatproof bowl; stand about 5 minutes or until liquid is absorbed, fluffing with fork occasionally, cool.
2 Boil, steam or microwave beans and peas, separately, until just tender; drain. Rinse under cold water; drain.
3 Combine mustard and oil in large bowl; add couscous, beans, peas and chives, toss gently.

----

prep & cook time 25 minutes (+ cooling) **serves** 8
nutritional count per serving 7.2g total fat
(1g saturated fat); 748kJ (179 cal);
22g carbohydrate; 5.2g protein; 2.2g fibre

Prepare the couscous and cook the beans and peas the day before the picnic. Plunging the barely cooked beans and peas into a bowl of iced water will instantly stop the cooking and will hold the colour better than rinsing them under cold water. Drain them well then wrap in paper towel and store in the fridge. Assemble the salad on the morning of the picnic.

Soak skewers in water for at least an hour before using to prevent scorching during cooking. These skewers are good served hot or cold. The paste can be made three days ahead (or even longer if frozen). The chicken can be skewered then coated in paste and kept, refrigerated, for up to a day before the picnic. Cook the skewers on the morning of the picnic.

chilli chicken skewers with coriander

1 long green chilli, chopped finely
1 small white onion (80g), quartered
2 cloves garlic, quartered
1 tablespoon ground coriander
1 tablespoon lemon juice
2 tablespoons olive oil
8 chicken thigh fillets (1.6kg), cut into 3cm pieces
¼ cup firmly packed fresh coriander leaves

1 Preheat oven to 220°C/200°C fan-forced. Line oven trays with baking paper.
2 Blend or process chilli, onion, garlic, ground coriander, juice and oil until mixture forms a smooth paste.
3 Combine chicken and paste in medium bowl; thread onto 16 skewers. Place skewers on oven trays, in single layer; bake about 20 minutes or until cooked through. Serve with fresh coriander leaves.

----

prep & cook time 40 minutes **serves** 8
nutritional count per serving 19g total fat (5g saturated fat); 1350kJ (323 cal); 0.8g carbohydrate; 37.5g protein; 0.4g fibre

Beetroot will discolour your skin, so use disposable gloves when handling it. Baby carrots are also called dutch carrots, it's rarely necessary to peel them. Prepare beetroot, carrots and the yogurt mixture the day before the picnic. Assemble salad at serving time.

baby carrot and fresh beetroot salad

800g baby carrots, trimmed
2 large beetroot (400g), grated coarsely
¼ cup (70g) yogurt
1 teaspoon ground cumin
1 tablespoon finely chopped fresh mint
2 tablespoons orange juice
1 tablespoon olive oil

1   Boil, steam or microwave carrots until tender; drain. Rinse under cold water, drain.
2   Squeeze excess moisture from beetroot.
3   Combine yogurt, cumin, mint, juice and oil in small bowl.
4   Serve vegetables drizzled with yogurt mixture.

----

prep & cook time 25 minutes **serves** 8
nutritional count per serving 2.6g total fat
(0.4g saturated fat); 318kJ (76 cal);
9.2g carbohydrate; 2g protein; 3.9g fibre

Cakes can be made and glazed up to two days before the picnic. Keep them in an airtight container at room temperature.

ginger cakes with orange glaze

⅔ cup (100g) plain flour
⅔ cup (100g) self-raising flour
½ teaspoon bicarbonate of soda
2 teaspoons ground cinnamon
2 teaspoons ground ginger
½ teaspoon ground cloves
1 cup (220g) firmly packed brown sugar
⅔ cup (160ml) buttermilk
2 eggs, beaten lightly
100g unsalted butter, melted
orange glaze
1 cup (160g) icing sugar
½ teaspoon finely grated orange rind
1 tablespoon strained orange juice
2 teaspoons hot water

1 Preheat oven to 180°C/160°C fan-forced. Grease and flour 8 holes of two 6-hole (¾-cup/180ml) mini fluted tube pans.
2 Sift flours, soda, spices and sugar into medium bowl, add buttermilk, egg and butter; stir until smooth. Divide mixture among pan holes; bake about 30 minutes.
3 Turn cakes immediately onto greased wire rack placed over tray. Cool.
4 Make orange glaze.
5 Pour glaze over cakes; stand until glaze is set.
orange glaze Sift icing sugar into medium bowl, add remaining ingredients; stir until smooth.

----

prep & cook time 45 minutes (+ standing) **makes** 8
nutritional count per cake 12.6g total fat
(7.6g saturated fat); 1639kJ (392 cal);
65.8g carbohydrate; 5.5g protein; 1g fibre

FRENCH COUNTRY PICNICS menu one

tomato, zucchini and anchovy tarts

12 small grape tomatoes (60g), halved
1½ sheets ready-rolled shortcrust pastry
1 medium zucchini (120g), grated coarsely
4 anchovy fillets, chopped finely
1 teaspoon fresh thyme leaves
2 eggs
⅓ cup (80ml) cream

1   Preheat oven to 160°C/140°C fan-forced.
2   Place tomato, cut-side up, on wire rack over oven tray. Roast, uncovered, 20 minutes. Cool.
3   Meanwhile, oil 12-hole (2-tablespoons/40ml) deep flat-based patty pan. Cut 12 x 7.5cm rounds from pastry; press into pan holes.
4   Increase oven temperature to 200°C/180°C fan-forced.
5   Squeeze excess moisture from zucchini. Combine zucchini, anchovy and thyme in small bowl. Divide mixture into pastry cases.

6   Whisk eggs and cream in small jug; pour into pastry cases, top with tomato, cut-side up. Bake about 25 minutes. Stand tarts in pan 5 minutes before removing from pan.

----

prep & cook time 55 minutes (+ cooling) **makes** 12
nutritional count per tart 9.6g total fat
(5.1g saturated fat); 577kJ (138 cal);
9.7g carbohydrate; 3.2g protein; 0.6g fibre

Roast the tomatoes and prepare the pastry cases the day before the picnic. Bake the tarts in the morning of the picnic.

Make the terrine up to two days ahead of the picnic. Slice the terrine before departure time or, better still, at the picnic.

chicken terrine

14 slices prosciutto (210g)
600g chicken thigh fillets
600g chicken breast fillets
¼ cup (35g) unsalted pistachios, chopped coarsely
3 teaspoons dijon mustard
1 teaspoon finely grated lemon rind
¼ cup coarsely chopped fresh flat-leaf parsley

1   Preheat oven to 200°C/180°C fan-forced. Oil 8cm x 20cm (5-cup/1.25-litre) loaf pan; line base and two long sides with baking paper, extending paper 5cm over sides.
2   Line base and sides of pan with prosciutto, slightly overlapping the slices and allowing overhang on long sides of pan.
3   Chop chicken into 2cm pieces. Process half the chicken until minced finely. Combine mince, remaining chopped chicken, nuts, mustard, rind and parsley in large bowl. Press chicken mixture into pan. Fold prosciutto slices over to cover chicken mixture. Fold baking paper over prosciutto; cover pan tightly with foil.
4   Place pan in medium baking dish. Pour in enough boiling water to come half way up side of pan. Bake terrine 1 hour. Carefully drain juices from pan. Cool, then weight with another dish filled with heavy cans.
5   Turn terrine onto plate; slice thickly to serve.

----

prep & cook time 1 hour 20 minutes (+ refrigeration)
serves 8
nutritional count per serving 13.3g total fat (3.7g saturated fat); 1116kJ (267 cal); 0.8g carbohydrate; 35.7g protein; 0.5g fibre

Make the dressing, and prepare, wash and dry the greens the day before the picnic. Assemble and dress the salad at the picnic.

roquefort and witlof salad

3 witlof (375g), leaves separated
1 bunch baby endive (250g), leaves separated
80g packet melba toasts, crushed lightly
150g Roquefort cheese, crumbled
dijon dressing
1 tablespoon dijon mustard
¼ cup (60ml) white wine vinegar
¼ cup (60ml) olive oil
pinch caster sugar
1 tablespoon water

1 Make dijon dressing.
2 Combine witlof, endive, toast and cheese in large bowl; drizzle with dijon dressing.
dijon dressing Combine ingredients in screw-top jar; shake well.

----

prep time 10 minutes **serves** 8
nutritional count per serving 13.3g total fat (4.9g saturated fat); 711kJ (170 cal); 6.2g carbohydrate; 5.6g protein; 1.7g fibre

Prepare watercress and combine remaining ingredients in a jar. Keep all these in the refrigerator the night before the picnic. Assemble the salad at the picnic.

roasted mushroom and watercress salad

400g swiss brown mushrooms, halved
1 tablespoon fresh thyme leaves
2 cloves garlic, crushed
2 tablespoons sherry vinegar
½ cup (125ml) olive oil
3 cups firmly packed watercress sprigs

1 Preheat oven to 220°C/200°C fan-forced.
2 Combine mushrooms, thyme, garlic, vinegar and oil in oiled shallow medium baking dish.
3 Roast mushrooms, uncovered, about 20 minutes or until mushrooms are tender. Cool.
4 Combine mushrooms and their juice in large bowl with watercress.

---

prep & cook time 30 minutes **serves** 8
nutritional count per serving 14.4g total fat (2g saturated fat); 606kJ (145 cal); 0.9g carbohydrate; 2.3g protein; 1.9g fibre

It's important to pack as many pieces of the apple into the tins as possible; the apples shrink during cooking. Golden delicious apples are the best for this recipe, but granny smith will do the job, too. The tarts are best made on the morning of the picnic; turn out of the tins onto a serving plate at the picnic. The pie is at its best after it's been removed from the oven for 1 hour. Instead of making two smaller tarte tartins you could make one larger one. If doing so, reduce pastry sheets to two and cut into a 23cm round and use a 22cm-round metal pie tin.

apple tarte tartin

6 medium golden delicious apples (900g)
2 tablespoons lemon juice
4 sheets ready-rolled puff pastry
1 cup (220g) caster sugar
100g unsalted butter, chopped coarsely
¼ cup (60ml) water

1 Preheat oven to 200°C/180°C fan-forced.
2 Peel, core and quarter apples; combine apples and juice in medium bowl.
3 Brush two pastry sheets with water; top with remaining sheets, press sheets firmly together. Cut an 18cm round from both pastry sheets.
4 Combine sugar, butter and the water in medium frying pan; stir over heat until sugar dissolves. Bring to the boil; reduce heat, simmer, without stirring, about 15 minutes, shaking pan occasionally, until dark caramel in colour. Allow bubbles to subside, carefully pour caramel into two shallow 16cm-round fluted metal pie tins. Add ¼ cup water to the hot frying pan; reserve caramel.

5 Position apple quarters in tins. Cut any remaining apples in half and place in tins to fill in any gaps.
6 Brush apples with reserved caramel; cover tarts with foil, bake 15 minutes.
7 Remove foil from tarts; carefully top apples with pastry rounds, tuck pastry down between the side of the tin and the apples. Bake about 30 minutes or until pastry is golden brown.
8 Stand 1 hour before turning onto serving plate.

----

prep & cook time 1 hour 20 minutes (+ standing)
serves 8
nutritional count per serving 23.8g total fat (7.8g saturated fat); 1935kJ (463 cal); 59.5g carbohydrate; 3.7g protein; 2.4g fibre

FRENCH COUNTRY PICNICS menu two

goats cheese, spinach and capsicum tarts
tuna, sour cream and chive dip
potato and green bean salad
chicken with tarragon cream
chocolate hazelnut cake

goats cheese, spinach and capsicum tarts

2 sheets ready-rolled puff pastry
4 large pieces roasted red capsicum (300g)
250g packet chopped frozen spinach, thawed
120g log goats cheese, crumbled
1 tablespoon olive oil
2 tablespoons basil pesto

1 Preheat oven to 220°C/200°C fan-forced. Line oven trays with baking paper.
2 Cut 8 x 9cm rounds from pastry; crimp edges of rounds to make borders; place on oven trays.

3 Cut capsicum pieces into rounds to fit inside pastry leaving a 5mm border. Finely chop remaining capsicum.
4 Squeeze excess moisture from spinach. Top capsicum with spinach, cheese and chopped capsicum; drizzle with oil.
5 Bake tarts about 15 minutes. Cool; top tarts with pesto.

----

prep & cook time 30 minutes (+ cooling) **makes** 8
nutritional count per tart 14.4g total fat
(3g saturated fat); 849kJ (203 cal);
12.4g carbohydrate; 5.3g protein; 2g fibre

Buy roasted capsicum from the deli.
Make the tarts on the day of the picnic.

perfect picnics french country picnics

57

tuna, sour cream and chive dip

125g packet cream cheese, softened
185g can tuna chunks in olive oil, drained
1 tablespoon horseradish cream
1 tablespoon lemon juice
¼ cup (60g) sour cream
pinch caster sugar
2 tablespoons finely chopped fresh chives
½ teaspoon finely grated lemon rind
2 x 125g boxes grissini (bread sticks)

1   Blend or process cream cheese, tuna, horseradish, juice, sour cream and sugar until smooth. Stir in chives and rind.
2   Sprinkle dip with some extra chives; serve with grissini.

prep time 15 minutes **serves** 8
nutritional count per serving 11.6g total fat (5.4g saturated fat); 995kJ (238 cal); 22.8g carbohydrate; 9.9g protein; 1.6g fibre

Make the dip the day before the picnic; cover and refrigerate until departure time.

potato and green bean salad

6 medium potatoes (650g), unpeeled
1 tablespoon olive oil
1 cup (180g) baby black olives, seeded
250g green beans, trimmed, halved
thyme vinaigrette
¼ cup (60ml) olive oil
2 tablespoons white wine vinegar
pinch caster sugar
1 clove garlic, crushed
2 teaspoons fresh lemon thyme leaves

1 Preheat oven to 200°C/180°C fan-forced.
2 Make thyme vinaigrette.
3 Quarter potatoes lengthways. Combine potatoes and oil in large baking dish; roast, uncovered, about 1 hour or until tender. Add hot potatoes and olives to thyme vinaigrette. Cool.
4 Meanwhile, boil, steam or microwave beans until tender; drain. Refresh under cold water; drain.
5 Mix beans into potato mixture.
thyme vinaigrette Whisk ingredients in large bowl.

prep & cook time 1 hour 15 minutes **serves** 8
nutritional count per serving 10g total fat
(1.4g saturated fat); 711kJ (170 cal);
15.7g carbohydrate; 2.8g protein; 2.7g fibre

We used desiree potatoes for the salad.
Make the salad on the morning of the picnic.

Whole-egg mayonnaise gives the best flavour. The chicken and tarragon cream can be made the day before the picnic; keep, covered separately, in the refrigerator until departure time.

chicken with tarragon cream

8 chicken drumettes (560g)
8 chicken wingettes (440g)
1 medium red onion (170g), chopped finely
1 clove garlic, crushed
1 bay leaf
½ cup (125ml) dry white wine
½ cup (125ml) water

tarragon cream
¼ cup (60g) packaged cream cheese, softened
1 tablespoon coarsely chopped fresh tarragon
1 tablespoon lemon juice
¼ cup (75g) mayonnaise
2 tablespoons warm water

1 Make tarragon cream.
2 Cook chicken, in batches, in heated oiled large frying pan until browned all over.
3 Return chicken to pan; stir in onion, garlic and bay leaf then wine. Bring to the boil; boil, uncovered, 2 minutes. Add the water to pan; bring to the boil. Reduce heat; simmer, uncovered, until liquid is almost evaporated and chicken is cooked. Cool.
4 Serve chicken with tarragon cream.
tarragon cream Beat cream cheese until smooth; stir in remaining ingredients.

----

prep & cook time 25 minutes **serves** 8
nutritional count per serving 11.7g total fat
(3.9g saturated fat); 1003kJ (240 cal);
3.4g carbohydrate; 27.6g protein; 0.4g fibre

If you can't find drumettes and wingettes, buy eight chicken wings, chop off and discard the tips. Chop the remaining pieces in half at the joint.

chocolate hazelnut cake

150g unsalted butter, chopped coarsely
150g dark eating chocolate, chopped coarsely
5 eggs, separated
⅔ cup (150g) caster sugar
1½ cups (150g) hazelnut meal
⅓ cup (45g) roasted hazelnuts, chopped coarsely
chocolate ganache
⅓ cup (80ml) thickened cream
100g dark eating chocolate, chopped coarsely

1 Preheat oven to 160°C/140°C fan-forced. Grease deep 20cm-round cake pan; line base and sides with baking paper.
2 Combine butter and chocolate in small saucepan; stir over low heat until smooth. Cool 10 minutes.
3 Beat egg yolks and sugar in medium bowl with electric mixer until thick and pale; beat in chocolate mixture. Beat egg whites in small bowl with electric mixer until soft peaks form. Fold hazelnut meal into chocolate mixture, then fold in egg white, in two batches. Spoon mixture into pan; bake about 1½ hours.
4 Cool cake in pan. Turn cake, top-side down, onto serving plate.
5 Meanwhile, make chocolate ganache.
6 Spread cake with ganache; top with nuts.
chocolate ganache Bring cream to the boil in small saucepan. Remove from heat, add chocolate; stir until smooth. Stand 5 minutes before using.

----

prep & cook time 2 hours **serves** 8
nutritional count per serving 37.5g total fat (15.9g saturated fat); 2061kJ (493 cal); 32.1g carbohydrate; 8.2g protein; 2.3g fibre

The cake can be made a week ahead; keep, covered, in the refrigerator. Make and use the ganache a day before the picnic. Keep the cake in the refrigerator until departure time.

sangria
panini with chorizo and manchego
pork ribs with lemon and garlic
chickpea, tomato and capsicum salad
cherry syrup cake

MEDITERRANEAN PICNICS menu one

sangria

¼ cup (55g) caster sugar
½ cup (125ml) orange juice, strained
½ cup (125ml) orange-flavoured liqueur
1 medium orange (240g), quartered, sliced thinly
1 medium lemon (140g), quartered, sliced thinly
1 medium lime (80g), quartered, sliced thinly
750ml bottle chilled sparkling shiraz
300ml bottle chilled soda water

1   Combine sugar and juice in large jug; stir until
sugar dissolves. Add liqueur and fruit.
2   Add shiraz and soda water to jug, pour into
ice-filled glasses.

prep time 15 minutes **serves** 8
nutritional count per serving 0.1g total fat
(0g saturated fat); 723kJ (173 cal);
10.5g carbohydrate; 0.6g protein; 0.9g fibre

Use fresh orange juice, and either Cointreau or
Grand Marnier. Use a large jug or bottle with a
tight fitting lid to take fruit and liqueur mixture
to the picnic. Add shiraz and soda just before
serving. We served our sangria with sicilian olives
and marinated green olives.

Use a whole-egg mayonnaise for the best flavour. Manchego cheese is Spanish, it is available from specialist cheese stores and Spanish delicatessens. If you can't find it, use parmesan cheese instead. Use a vegetable peeler to shave the cheese.

panini with chorizo and manchego

3 smoked chorizo sausages (510g), sliced thickly
1 cup (280g) mayonnaise
½ teaspoon smoked paprika
8 panini rolls (800g)
5 hard-boiled eggs, sliced thinly
80g baby spinach leaves
150g manchego cheese, shaved

1 Cook chorizo in heated oiled large frying pan, in batches, until browned. Drain on absorbent paper.
2 Combine mayonnaise and paprika in small bowl.
3 Split panini in half; spread mayonnaise mixture over roll halves. Top with chorizo, egg, spinach, cheese and remaining panini half.

----

prep & cook time 20 minutes **makes** 8
nutritional count per serving 39.9g total fat
(12.6g saturated fat); 3018kJ (722 cal);
60.2g carbohydrate; 28.9g protein; 4.1g fibre

The racks can be marinated a day before the picnic; keep refrigerated. Cook and cut the racks on the morning of the picnic. Take lots of paper napkins for sticky fingers.

pork ribs with lemon and garlic

1 tablespoon sweet paprika
2 teaspoons finely grated lemon rind
⅓ cup (80ml) lemon juice
2 teaspoons thyme leaves
4 cloves garlic, crushed
2 tablespoons honey
¼ cup (60ml) vegetable oil
2kg racks american-style pork spare ribs

1 Preheat oven to 240°C/220°C fan-forced. Line two oven trays with baking paper.
2 Combine paprika, rind, juice, thyme, garlic, honey and oil in large bowl; add racks, rub all over with paprika mixture.
3 Place racks on trays. Bake about 30 minutes or until well browned.
4 Cut racks into individual ribs to serve.

----

prep & cook time 40 minutes **serves** 8
nutritional count per serving 20.2g total fat
(6.1g saturated fat); 1404kJ (336 cal);
6.3g carbohydrate; 32.4g protein; 0.3g fibre

chickpea, tomato and capsicum salad

⅓ cup (80ml) olive oil
3 medium red capsicums (600g), sliced thinly
2 cloves garlic, crushed
¼ cup (60ml) lemon juice
2 tablespoons red wine vinegar
400g can chickpeas, rinsed, drained
4 small tomatoes (360g), sliced thinly
1 cup coarsely chopped fresh flat-leaf parsley

1   Heat half the oil in large frying pan. Add capsicum and garlic; cook, stirring, about 5 minutes or until capsicum softens. Cool.
2   Combine capsicum, remaining oil, juice, vinegar, chickpeas, tomato and parsley in large bowl; toss gently. Serve with lemon wedges.

----

prep & cook time 20 minutes (+ cooling) **serves** 8
nutritional count per serving 10g total fat
(1.4g saturated fat); 606kJ (145 cal);
8.2g carbohydrate; 3.8g protein; 3.3g fibre

Cook the capsicum mixture the day before the picnic; keep, covered, in the fridge. The salad is best assembled on the morning of the picnic.

The cake can be made a day before the picnic. Slice the cake
and drizzle with the reserved syrup at the picnic.

cherry syrup cake

125g unsalted butter, softened
1 teaspoon finely grated lemon rind
¾ cup (165g) caster sugar
2 eggs
1¾ cups (260g) self-raising flour
¾ cup (180ml) buttermilk
cherry syrup
1 cup (220g) caster sugar
2 tablespoons lemon juice
½ cup (125ml) water
680g jar morello cherries, drained

1 Preheat oven to 170°C/150°C fan-forced. Grease
8cm x 20cm (5-cup/1.25-litre) loaf pan; line base and long
sides with baking paper, extending paper 5cm over sides.
2 Beat butter, rind and sugar in small bowl with electric
mixer until light and fluffy. Beat in eggs, one at a time.
Transfer mixture to large bowl; stir in sifted flour and
buttermilk, in two batches.
3 Spread mixture into pan; bake about 1 hour. Stand cake
in pan 5 minutes before turning, top-side up, onto wire
rack placed over oven tray; remove baking paper. Cool.
4 Meanwhile, make cherry syrup.
5 Slowly spoon hot syrup and cherries over cake. Place
cake on plate; pour syrup from tray into jar.
6 Serve cake slices drizzled with remaining syrup.
cherry syrup Combine sugar, juice and the water in
medium saucepan. Stir over heat, without boiling, until
sugar dissolves; bring to the boil. Boil, uncovered,
without stirring, 2 minutes. Add cherries, bring to the
boil; reduce heat, simmer 2 minutes.

----

prep & cook time 1 hour 30 minutes (+ cooling)
serves 8
nutritional count per serving 15.4g total fat
(9.4g saturated fat); 1998kJ (478 cal);
79.6g carbohydrate; 6.6g protein; 2g fibre

caramelised onion tarts
cumin roasted quail
white bean and tomato salad
tabbouleh with charred lamb
lemon panna cotta pots

MEDITERRANEAN PICNICS menu two

caramelised onion tarts

20g butter
1 tablespoon olive oil
2 large red onions (600g), halved, sliced thinly
1 tablespoon brown sugar
1 clove garlic, crushed
2 teaspoons thyme leaves
1 tablespoon red wine vinegar
2 tablespoons water
1 sheet ready-rolled puff pastry, halved
6 cherry bocconcini cheese (65g), sliced thickly

1 Preheat oven to 220°C/200°C fan-forced. Line oven tray with baking paper.
2 Melt butter with oil in large frying pan, add onion, sugar, garlic and half the thyme; cook over low heat about 20 minutes, stirring occasionally, until onion is very soft and browned lightly. Add vinegar and the water; cook, stirring, until liquid has evaporated.
3 Meanwhile, place pastry pieces on tray; prick all over with fork. Freeze 15 minutes.
4 Top pastry pieces with caramelised onion, leaving 1cm border; bake about 15 minutes or until browned. Cool.
5 Top tarts with cheese; cut each tart into four pieces; sprinkle with remaining thyme.

prep & cook time 40 minutes (+ freezing) **makes** 8
nutritional count per tart quarter 10.9g total fat
(3.1g saturated fat); 702kJ (169 cal);
13.2g carbohydrate; 4.2g protein; 1.3g fibre

Caramelised onion can be made a day before the picnic; keep, covered, in the refrigerator. Finish making the tarts on the morning of the picnic.

cumin roasted quail

6 x 160g quail
1 tablespoon ground cumin
1 teaspoon dried chilli flakes
2 cloves garlic, crushed
2 tablespoons olive oil
1 tablespoon lemon juice
½ cup loosely packed fresh coriander leaves

1 Preheat oven to 220°C/200°C fan-forced.
2 Rinse quails under cold water; pat dry, inside and out, with absorbent paper. Using kitchen scissors, cut along each side of quails' backbones; discard backbones, cut quails in half. Combine quail, cumin, chilli, garlic, oil and juice in large bowl, cover; refrigerate 3 hours or overnight.

3 Place quail, skin-side up, in single layer, in large baking dish; bake about 20 minutes or until cooked through. Cool.
4 Serve quail sprinkled with coriander.

----

prep & cook time 25 minutes (+ refrigeration & cooling)
serves 8
nutritional count per serving 11.2g total fat (2.4g saturated fat); 606kJ (145 cal); 0.1g carbohydrate; 11.2g protein; 0.1g fibre

Quail can be bought already boned, but with the bones remaining in the legs and wings. Ask the butcher or poultry shop to remove any remaining bones for you, if you like. We've chosen to leave all the bones intact in the recipe. Quail can be prepared for cooking a day ahead of the picnic; bake the quail on the morning of the picnic.

white bean and tomato salad

2 x 400g cans cannellini beans, rinsed, drained

2 medium tomatoes (300g), quartered, seeded, sliced thinly

¼ cup firmly packed fresh oregano leaves

1 small red onion (100g), chopped finely

2 tablespoons lemon juice

¼ cup (60ml) olive oil

½ cup (60g) seeded black olives, chopped coarsely

1   Combine ingredients in large bowl; toss gently.

----

prep time 15 minutes **serves** 8

nutritional count per serving 7.3g total fat
(1g saturated fat); 518kJ (124 cal);
9.4g carbohydrate; 3.9g protein; 3.6g fibre

Salad can be made a day before the picnic;
keep covered in the refrigerator.

The cutlets can be marinated overnight then cooked on the morning of the picnic. The tabbouleh is best made on the morning of the picnic.

tabbouleh with charred lamb

1 clove garlic, crushed
1 tablespoon dijon mustard
1 tablespoon lemon juice
2 tablespoons olive oil
8 french-trimmed lamb cutlets (400g)

tabbouleh

½ cup (80g) burghul
⅓ cup (80ml) boiling water
1 cup firmly packed fresh mint leaves, chopped finely
1 cup firmly packed fresh flat-leaf parsley leaves, chopped finely
6 green onions, chopped finely
¼ cup (60ml) lemon juice
¼ cup (60ml) olive oil

1 Combine garlic, mustard, juice and oil with lamb in medium bowl.
2 Cook lamb on heated oiled grill plate (or grill or barbecue) until cooked to your liking. Cool.
3 Make tabbouleh.
4 Serve lamb with tabbouleh.

tabbouleh Place burghul in large heatproof bowl, add the water; cover, stand 5 minutes or until water is absorbed. Stir in remaining ingredients.

----

prep & cook time 25 minutes (+ standing & cooling)
serves 8
nutritional count per serving 12.9g total fat (2.7g saturated fat); 711kJ (170 cal); 3.8g carbohydrate; 6.7g protein; 1.6g fibre

Panna cotta is best made the day before the picnic. Keep chilled until ready to eat. If you like, serve fresh fruit, such as berries or stone fruit, with the panna cotta.

lemon panna cotta pots

1 litre (4 cups) thickened cream
3 teaspoons gelatine
¾ cup (165g) caster sugar
½ teaspoon vanilla extract
1 teaspoon finely grated lemon rind
2 tablespoons lemon juice

1 Grease eight ⅔-cup (160ml) plastic dariole moulds or teacups.
2 Pour cream into medium saucepan, add gelatine, sugar and extract; stir over heat, without boiling, until gelatine and sugar dissolve.

3 Strain mixture into large jug; stir in rind and juice. Cool.
4 Pour mixture into moulds; cover, refrigerate 4 hours or overnight.
5 Serve lemon panna cotta in moulds.

----

prep & cook time 15 minutes (+ cooling & refrigeration)
serves 8
nutritional count per serving 46.5g total fat
(30.6g saturated fat); 2182kJ (522 cal);
24.7g carbohydrate; 3.1g protein; 0g fibre

oysters with tomato and shallot vinaigrette
smoked trout ribbon sandwich
prosciutto, melon and mustard ribbon sandwich
potted prawns with crostini
baby pea and fetta rice cakes
mochaccino tartlets

ROMANTIC PICNICS menu one

oysters with tomato and shallot vinaigrette

2 teaspoons red wine vinegar
1 tablespoon olive oil
½ small shallot (15g), chopped finely
1 small tomato (90g), seeded, chopped finely
1 teaspoon finely chopped fresh flat-leaf parsley
8 oysters, on the half shell

1   Combine vinegar, oil, shallot, tomato and parsley
in screw-top jar; shake well.
2   Top oysters with vinaigrette.

prep time 10 minutes **serves** 2
nutritional count per serving 10.6g total fat
(1.8g saturated fat); 543kJ (130 cal);
1g carbohydrate; 7.6g protein; 0.3g fibre

Make sure the oysters you buy are freshly shucked,
and keep them well-iced on the way to the picnic.
Take the dressing to the picnic in the screw-top jar.
Use either a red shallot or the french golden variety, and
use a full-flavoured tomato – vine-ripened is good.

smoked trout ribbon sandwich

2 tablespoons mayonnaise
½ teaspoon finely grated lemon rind
1 teaspoon lemon juice
2 teaspoons finely chopped fresh chives
4 slices square multigrain bread (180g)
70g skinless smoked trout, flaked finely

1   Combine mayonnaise, rind, juice and chives in small bowl.
2   Spread bread with mayonnaise mixture. Sandwich trout between bread slices. Trim crusts; cut each sandwich into three fingers.

----

prep time 10 minutes **serves** 2
nutritional count per serving 10.8g total fat (1.4g saturated fat); 1446kJ (346 cal); 42.4g carbohydrate; 17.3g protein; 4.5g fibre

Use a good quality whole-egg mayonnaise.

prosciutto, melon and mustard ribbon sandwich

80g spreadable cream cheese, softened
2 teaspoons wholegrain mustard
4 slices square white bread (180g)
2 slices prosciutto (30g), halved crossways
¼ small rockmelon (300g), sliced thinly

1   Combine cream cheese and mustard in small bowl.
2   Spread bread with cream cheese mixture. Sandwich prosciutto and melon between bread slices. Trim crusts; cut each sandwich into three fingers.

----

prep time 10 minutes **serves** 2
nutritional count per serving 16.6g total fat (9.2g saturated fat); 1676kJ (401 cal); 46.5g carbohydrate; 14.4g protein; 3.8g fibre

Sandwiches can be made up to two hours before the picnic.

potted prawns with crostini

300g uncooked tiger prawns
125g unsalted butter, melted
¼ teaspoon mustard powder
1 tablespoon finely chopped fresh chives
cooking-oil spray
1 small french breadstick (150g), sliced thinly

1 Preheat oven to 200°C/180°C fan-forced.
2 Shell and devein prawns. Cook prawns in small saucepan of boiling water until changed in colour; drain. Rinse under cold water; drain.
3 Process prawns, butter and mustard until almost smooth; stir in chives.

4 Divide mixture between two ½-cup (125ml) ramekins, cover, refrigerate about 1 hour or until set.
5 Meanwhile, to make crostini, spray both sides of bread slices with oil, place on oven tray; toast in oven until browned lightly.
6 Serve potted prawns with crostini.

----

prep & cook time 25 minutes (+ refrigeration) **serves** 2
nutritional count per serving 57.3g total fat
(34.9g saturated fat); 3202kJ (766 cal);
40.2g carbohydrate; 22.5g protein; 2.8g fibre

Potted prawns can be made a day before the picnic, keep well-iced during transportation. Make crostini close to departure time.

baby pea and fetta rice cakes

¼ cup (50g) white long-grain rice
⅓ cup (40g) frozen baby green peas, thawed
1 tablespoon finely chopped fresh flat-leaf parsley
2 eggs, beaten lightly
1 tablespoon milk
40g fetta cheese, crumbled

1 Preheat oven to 180°C/160°C fan-forced. Oil four holes of 12-hole (½-cup/125ml) oval friand pan; line bases with baking paper.
2 Cook rice in saucepan of boiling water until tender. Drain, rinse under cold water; drain well.

3 Combine rice and remaining ingredients in medium bowl.
4 Divide mixture into pan holes; bake 25 minutes.
5 Stand rice cakes in pan 5 minutes before turning, top-side up, onto wire rack to cool.

----

prep & cook time 45 minutes **serves** 2
nutritional count per serving 11.2g total fat (5.2g saturated fat); 1041kJ (249 cal); 22.1g carbohydrate; 14.3g protein; 1.5g fibre

Rice cakes are best made on the day of the picnic.

The tart cases we used were bought frozen and unbaked; they come ready-to-bake in foil cases and measure 6.5cm in diameter. They are available from supermarkets. Tartlets can be made a day ahead, keep refrigerated.

mochaccino tartlets

6 frozen unbaked sweet tart cases (130g)
80g dark eating chocolate, chopped coarsely
2 tablespoons cream
1 teaspoon instant coffee granules
2 teaspoons coffee-flavoured liqueur
2 egg yolks
1 tablespoon caster sugar
2 teaspoons cocoa powder

1 Preheat oven to 180°C/160°C fan-forced.
2 Place tart cases on greased and lined oven tray; bake about 12 minutes. Cool.
3 Combine chocolate, cream, coffee and liqueur in small heatproof bowl placed over small saucepan of simmering water; stir until smooth. Remove bowl from pan; cool 5 minutes.
4 Whisk egg yolks and sugar in small bowl until creamy; fold in chocolate mixture.
5 Divide filling into cases. Bake, in oven, 8 minutes; cool 5 minutes. Refrigerate 20 minutes before serving.
6 Serve tartlets dusted with sifted cocoa.

----

prep & cook time 30 minutes (+ refrigeration) **makes** 6
nutritional count per tartlet 14.7g total fat
(8.2g saturated fat); 999kJ (239 cal);
23g carbohydrate; 3.4g protein; 0.6g fibre

ROMANTIC PICNICS menu two

peking duck pancakes

¼ chinese barbecued duck (250g)
2 green onions, trimmed
10g snow pea sprouts
6 frozen peking duck pancakes, thawed
¼ cup (60ml) hoisin sauce

1 Remove and discard bones from duck, slice meat thinly. Cut onions in half lengthways; cut crossways into three pieces. Cut sprouts in half crossways.
2 Heat pancakes following packet instructions.
3 Divide duck, onion, sprouts and sauce over pancakes; roll to enclose.

----

prep time 15 minutes **serves** 2
nutritional count per serving 20.9g total fat
(5.9g saturated fat); 1450kJ (347 cal);
21.9g carbohydrate; 16.6g protein; 4.1g fibre

Chinese barbecued ducks can be bought from Asian butchers or some Chinese supermarkets or restaurants. Peking duck pancakes can be found in the freezer section of Asian supermarkets. Assemble the pancakes before you leave for the picnic.

peking duck pancakes
thai beef salad
green tea noodle salad
honey and fig damper with cheese selection
white chocolate truffles

Assemble the salad at the picnic.

thai beef salad

200g lean beef rump steak
1 shallot (25g), sliced thinly
1 fresh long red chilli, chopped finely
1 cup (80g) bean sprouts
1 kaffir lime leaf, shredded finely
½ cup firmly packed fresh coriander leaves
½ cup fresh mint leaves
thai salad dressing
2 tablespoons lime juice
2 tablespoons fish sauce
pinch caster sugar
2 teaspoons peanut oil

1 Make thai salad dressing.
2 Cook beef on heated oiled grill plate (or grill or barbecue) about 5 minutes or until cooked to your liking. Cover beef; stand 10 minutes then slice thinly.
3 Combine beef, remaining ingredients and dressing in large bowl.
thai salad dressing Combine ingredients in screw-top jar; shake well.

prep & cook time 20 minutes **serves** 2
nutritional count per serving 14.6g total fat (5.2g saturated fat); 1058kJ (253 cal); 3.9g carbohydrate; 24.5g protein; 2.9g fibre

Add dressing to salad at the picnic. We bought a 200g packet of green-tea flavoured noodles from an Asian supermarket to use in this recipe.

green tea noodle salad

80g green tea noodles
4 green onions, sliced thinly
50g snow pea sprouts, chopped coarsely
coconut dressing
2 tablespoons coconut milk
1 tablespoon mirin
2 tablespoons rice wine vinegar
1 tablespoon peanut oil

1 Make coconut dressing.
2 Cook noodles in large saucepan of boiling water until tender; drain. Rinse under cold water; drain.
3 Combine noodles, remaining ingredients and dressing in large bowl.
coconut dressing Combine ingredients in screw-top jar; shake well.

----

prep & cook time 15 minutes **serves** 2
nutritional count per serving 13.9g total fat (5.4g saturated fat); 1279kJ (306 cal); 34.5g carbohydrate; 7.2g protein; 3g fibre

honey and fig damper with cheese selection

1½ cups (225g) self-raising flour
25g cold butter, chopped coarsely
¾ cup (180ml) buttermilk
4 dried figs (60g), chopped finely
1 tablespoon honey
1 tablespoon self-raising flour, extra

1 Preheat oven to 220°C/200°C fan-forced.
2 Sift flour into bowl; rub in butter. Add buttermilk, figs and honey to flour mixture; mix to a soft dough. Turn dough onto floured surface; knead lightly until smooth.
3 Shape dough into 8cm x 24cm log; place on greased oven tray. Dust log with extra sifted flour; cut slashes into top of log.

4 Bake damper 10 minutes. Reduce oven temperature to 180°C/160°C fan-forced; bake about 10 minutes. Lift damper onto wire rack, cover; cool.
5 Serve damper with a selection of cheeses, butter and figs, if you like.

----

prep & cook time 30 minutes (+ cooling) **serves** 2
nutritional count per serving (damper only)
13.7g total fat (8.2g saturated fat); 2817kJ (674 cal); 116.4g carbohydrate; 16.7g protein; 8.8g fibre

Damper is best made on the day of the picnic. Serve the damper with your favourite cheeses, or try a soft blue cheese and a brie.

white chocolate truffles

1½ tablespoons cream
60g white eating chocolate, chopped coarsely
¼ cup (35g) unsalted pistachios, chopped finely
1 teaspoon coconut-flavoured liqueur
120g white chocolate Melts
1 tablespoon finely chopped unsalted pistachios, extra

1   Combine cream and chocolate in small heatproof bowl; stir over small saucepan of simmering water until smooth (do not let water touch base of bowl). Remove bowl from pan, stir in nuts and liqueur. Cover; refrigerate until firm.
2   Roll level teaspoons of mixture into balls, place on baking-paper-lined tray. Cover; refrigerate until firm.
3   Stir Melts in small heatproof bowl over small saucepan of simmering water until smooth (do not let water touch base of bowl). Remove bowl from pan. Dip chocolate balls into melted chocolate, place on baking- paper-lined tray; sprinkle with extra nuts. Cover; refrigerate until firm.

----

prep & cook time 20 minutes (+ refrigeration) **serves** 2
nutritional count per serving 47.5g total fat
(24.2g saturated fat); 2851kJ (682 cal);
54.2g carbohydrate; 11.1g protein; 2g fibre

Truffles can be made two days ahead of the picnic; keep cool.

corn cakes with avocado smash
lemon pepper chicken drumettes
cheese and vegie sandwiches
minted melon salad
chocolate blueberry slab cake

KIDS' PICNICS menu one

corn cakes with avocado smash

2 corn cobs (800g), trimmed
2 teaspoons olive oil
3 green onions, sliced thinly
2 tablespoons self-raising flour
¼ teaspoon bicarbonate of soda
2 eggs, beaten lightly
⅓ cup (80ml) light sour cream
avocado smash
1 medium avocado (250g), chopped coarsely
1 tablespoon lime juice

1 Cut kernels from corn cobs.
2 Heat oil in large frying pan; cook corn and onion, stirring, until onion softens. Cool.
3 Combine corn mixture, sifted flour and soda, and egg in medium bowl.

4 Heat oiled large frying pan, drop rounded tablespoons of mixture, in batches, into pan; cook about 1 minute each side.
5 Make avocado smash.
6 Serve corn cakes topped with smash and sour cream.
avocado smash Combine ingredients in small bowl; mash with fork.

---

prep & cook time 30 minutes **makes** 8
nutritional count per serving 10.5g total fat
(3.1g saturated fat); 769kJ (184 cal);
14.4g carbohydrate; 6g protein; 3.7g fibre

Prepare the corn mixture the day before the picnic.
Make the corn cakes on the morning of the picnic.
Prepare the avocado smash as close to departure time
as possible; cover the surface with plastic wrap.

lemon pepper chicken drumettes

16 chicken drumettes (1kg)
1 teaspoon finely grated lemon rind
2 tablespoons lemon juice
1 teaspoon cracked black pepper
1 tablespoon olive oil
¼ teaspoon ground turmeric
¼ teaspoon sweet paprika

1 Preheat oven to 200°C/180°C fan-forced. Line large baking dish with baking paper.
2 Combine chicken with remaining ingredients in medium bowl.
3 Place chicken, in single layer, in pan; bake, uncovered, about 40 minutes or until cooked through. Cool.

prep & cook time 50 minutes **serves** 8
nutritional count per serving 9g total fat
(2.5g saturated fat); 835kJ (199 cal);
0.1g carbohydrate; 29.2g protein; 0g fibre

Chicken can be cooked, cooled and refrigerated a day before the picnic.

cheese and vegie sandwiches

1 medium carrot (120g), grated coarsely
2 small zucchini (180g), grated coarsely
2 green onions, sliced thinly
1 cup (120g) coarsely grated cheddar cheese
⅓ cup (100g) mayonnaise
8 slices soy and linseed sandwich loaf (360g)
40g butter, softened

1 Combine vegetables, cheese and mayonnaise in medium bowl.
2 Spread bread with butter. Sandwich vegetable mixture between bread slices.
3 Remove crusts; cut sandwiches in half.

prep time 20 minutes **makes** 8
nutritional count per serving 14.6g total fat
(6.5g saturated fat); 1095kJ (262 cal);
22.8g carbohydrate; 8.5g protein; 3g fibre

Prepare the vegies and cheese the day before the picnic; store, separately, in the fridge. Drain zucchini well before making the sandwiches on the morning of the picnic. Use your favourite mayonnaise – we like the whole-egg variety. Use butter or your favourite spread for the sandwiches, although this filling is moist enough without a spread. Don't season the vegies with salt, it will draw the moisture from the zucchini, which will make the sandwiches soggy.

Use any combination of melons you like. Prepare the melons a day before the picnic, keep them, covered, in the fridge. Add mint and juice to the melons at the picnic.

minted melon salad

½ small rockmelon (650g)
1 small honeydew melon (1.3kg)
1kg piece seedless watermelon
¼ cup loosely packed fresh mint leaves
½ cup (125ml) apple juice

1 Discard seeds from rockmelon and honeydew. Using melon baller, scoop balls from melons into large bowl.
2 Chop watermelon into small chunks, add to bowl. Stir in mint and juice.

----

prep time 20 minutes **serves** 8
nutritional count per serving 0.6g total fat
(0g saturated fat); 326kJ (78 cal);
15.7g carbohydrate; 1.3g protein; 2.2g fibre

chocolate blueberry slab cake

½ cup (50g) cocoa powder
½ cup (125ml) boiling water
160g unsalted butter, softened
1½ cups (330g) caster sugar
3 eggs
1⅓ cups (200g) self-raising flour
⅓ cup (50g) plain flour
½ teaspoon bicarbonate of soda
¾ cup (180ml) buttermilk
⅔ cup (100g) fresh blueberries
chocolate icing
100g dark cooking chocolate, chopped coarsely
25g butter
1 cup (160g) icing sugar, sifted
1½ tablespoons hot water

1 Preheat oven to 180°C/160°C fan-forced. Grease 19cm x 30cm lamington pan; line with baking paper.
2 Blend cocoa with the water in small bowl. Cool.
3 Beat butter and sugar in small bowl with electric mixer until light and fluffy. Beat in eggs, one at a time. Transfer mixture to large bowl, stir in sifted flours and soda, and buttermilk in two batches; stir in cocoa mixture.
4 Spread mixture into pan. Bake about 30 minutes. Cool cake in pan 20 minutes before turning, top-side up, onto wire rack to cool.
5 Make chocolate icing.
6 Spread cold cake with icing; top with blueberries. Cut cake into squares.
chocolate icing Melt chocolate and butter in small saucepan, stirring, over low heat. Remove from heat; stir in sifted icing sugar and water until smooth.

----

prep & cook time 55 minutes (+ cooling) **makes** 20
nutritional count per piece 10.7g total fat
(6.5g saturated fat); 1083kJ (259 cal);
38.2g carbohydrate; 3.6g protein; 0.7g fibre

The cake can be completed a day before the picnic. The iced cake can be frozen for several weeks then topped with berries on the morning of the picnic. The cake can be thawed in the fridge the night before the picnic.

KIDS' PICNICS menu two

vegie hash brown heart puffs
mini cabanossi pizzas
ham, cheese and tomato chutney wraps
chocolate twists
coconut cupcakes

vegie hash brown heart puffs

1 large potato (300g), unpeeled
1 medium zucchini (120g), grated coarsely
1 medium carrot (120g), grated coarsely
1 small red capsicum (150g), sliced thinly
2 tablespoons self-raising flour
1 egg, beaten lightly

1 Boil, steam or microwave potato until tender. When potato is cool enough to handle, peel away skin, then coarsely grate into large bowl.
2 Squeeze excess moisture from zucchini, add to bowl with remaining ingredients; mix well.

3 Heat oiled large frying pan; drop rounded tablespoons of mixture into 7.5cm greased heart-shaped cutter, into pan. Cook until browned both sides and cooked through. Repeat with remaining mixture.

----

prep & cook time 30 minutes **makes** 12
nutritional count per puff 2.1g total fat
(0.4g saturated fat); 201kJ (48 cal);
5g carbohydrate; 1.7g protein; 0.9g fibre

Any firm potato can be used, we used desiree. The puffs are good eaten either hot or cold. The vegies can be prepared a day before the picnic, but the puffs need to be cooked on the morning of the picnic. If you don't want to use a heart-shaped cutter, simply drop rounded tablespoons of mixture into pan.

These are good eaten either warm or cold. Make the pizzas on the morning of the picnic

mini cabanossi pizzas

440g pizza base with sauce
1 medium zucchini (120g), grated coarsely
100g cabanossi, sliced thinly
12 cherry bocconcini cheese (130g)

1 Preheat oven to 220°C/200°C fan-forced. Line oven tray with baking paper.
2 Cut 12 x 6.5cm fluted rounds from pizza base; place on tray.
3 Top pizza rounds with zucchini, cabanossi and torn pieces of cheese. Bake about 5 minutes or until heated through.

----

prep & cook time 20 minutes **makes** 12
nutritional count per pizza 5.1g total fat (2.1g saturated fat); 644kJ (154 cal); 19.6g carbohydrate; 6.5g protein; 1.5g fibre

Prepare the wraps the night before the picnic; wrap each roll tightly in plastic wrap and refrigerate. Cut the rolls at the picnic.

ham, cheese and tomato chutney wraps

8 mountain bread squares (200g)
½ cup (160g) tomato chutney
50g baby spinach leaves
2 cups (250g) coarsely grated cheddar cheese
300g shaved leg ham

1 Place two bread slices together, spread with rounded tablespoons of chutney. Top each with spinach, cheese and ham; roll to enclose.
2 Cut rolls into thirds crossways to serve.

----

prep time 15 minutes makes 12
nutritional count per wrap 9.2g total fat
(5.2g saturated fat), 782kJ (187 cal);
13.9g carbohydrate; 11.7g protein; 1.2g fibre

chocolate twists

1 sheet ready-rolled puff pastry
2 tablespoons apple juice
100g milk chocolate Melts, melted

1 Preheat oven to 200°C/180°C fan-forced. Line oven tray with baking paper.
2 Cut pastry in half. Cut each half crossways into 2cm strips.
3 Place juice in small bowl. Dip pastry strips into juice, one at a time; twist each strip, place, in single layer, on tray. Bake about 10 minutes or until pastry is golden brown.
4 Dip one end of each pastry twist into melted chocolate, return to tray to set.

----

prep +cook time 25 minutes **makes 24**
nutritional count per twist 4.5g total fat
(1.1g saturated fat); 309kJ (74 cal);
7.5g carbohydrate; 1g protein; 0.2g fibre

Make the pastry twists a day before the picnic. Keep them in an airtight container at room temperature. If the weather is very hot, keep the twists in the fridge.

coconut cupcakes

125g unsalted butter, softened
1 teaspoon finely grated lemon rind
¾ cup (165g) caster sugar
2 eggs
½ cup (40g) desiccated coconut
1¼ cups (185g) self-raising flour
½ cup (125ml) milk
2 tablespoons desiccated coconut, extra
pink icing
1¼ cups (200g) icing sugar, sifted
1 tablespoon boiling water, approximately
pink food colouring

1 Preheat oven to 180°C/160°C fan-forced. Line 12-hole (⅓-cup/80ml) muffin pan with paper cases.
2 Beat butter, rind and sugar in small bowl with electric mixer until light and fluffy. Beat in eggs, one at a time. Transfer mixture to large bowl; stir in desiccated coconut, sifted flour, and milk in two batches.

3 Divide mixture into paper cases; bake about 30 minutes. Stand cupcakes in pan 5 minutes before turning, top-side up, onto wire rack to cool.
4 Make pink icing. Spread icing over cold cupcakes; sprinkle with extra coconut.
pink icing Sift icing sugar into small bowl; stir in enough water to make icing spreadable. Tint pink with colouring.

----

prep & cook time 1 hour 10 minutes (+ cooling)
makes 12
nutritional count per cupcake 13.1g total fat (8.8g saturated fat); 1238kJ (296 cal); 42.1g carbohydrate; 3.5g protein; 1.2g fibre

Make cakes a day before the picnic. Keep in an airtight container at room temperature. Uniced cupcakes can be frozen.

chipolatas with sweet chilli sauce
sticky tangy apricot chicken wings
rainbow rice salad
fruit skewers
carrot cakes with cream cheese frosting

KIDS' PICNICS menu three

chipolatas with sweet chilli sauce

8 lean beef chipolata sausages (240g)
8 mini oval dinner rolls (320g)
¼ cup (60ml) sweet chilli sauce
20g baby rocket leaves
¾ cup (90g) coarsely grated cheddar cheese

1 Cook sausages in oiled medium frying pan, cool.
2 Split rolls, spread with sauce; fill with rocket, cheese and sausages.

prep +cook time 20 minutes   makes 8
nutritional count per roll 12.3g total fat
(6g saturated fat); 1037kJ (248 cal);
23.3g carbohydrate; 9.8g protein; 2.5g fibre

Sausages can be cooked the day before the picnic. Keep in the fridge. Assemble rolls the morning of the picnic.

The wings can be prepared the day before the picnic, keep covered in the fridge. Cook the wings on the morning of the picnic – they're yummy hot or cold. The wings are sticky, so make sure you have a good supply of paper napkins for sticky fingers.

sticky apricot chicken wings

8 large chicken wings (800g)
⅓ cup (110g) apricot jam
1 teaspoon sweet paprika
2 tablespoons lemon juice
1 tablespoon olive oil
1 tablespoon finely chopped fresh chives

1   Preheat oven to 200°C/180°C fan-forced.
2   Combine wings with jam, paprika, juice and oil in large bowl.
3   Place undrained wings, in single layer, in large baking dish. Roast, uncovered, about 35 minutes or until cooked through. Cool. Sprinkle with chives.

----

prep & cook time 45 minutes (+ cooling) **makes** 8
nutritional count per serving 5.6g total fat (1.4g saturated fat); 606kJ (145 cal); 9.2g carbohydrate; 14.5g protein; 0.2g fibre

rainbow rice salad

1¼ cups (250g) basmati rice
2 tablespoons olive oil
2 teaspoons dijon mustard
2 tablespoons lemon juice
420g can corn kernels, rinsed, drained
1 medium red capsicum (200g), chopped finely
⅓ cup (40g) seeded black olives, chopped coarsely
½ cup coarsely chopped fresh flat-leaf parsley

1   Cook rice in large saucepan of boiling water until tender, drain; rinse under cold water, drain.
2   Whisk oil, mustard and juice in large bowl. Gently mix in rice and remaining ingredients.

----

prep & cook time 25 minutes **serves** 8
nutritional count per serving 5.4g total fat
(0.7g saturated fat); 861kJ (206 cal);
34.2g carbohydrate; 3.8g protein; 2g fibre

Use any rice you like for this recipe, just make sure it's cooked properly so every grain is separate. You could use about 3½ cups of cold leftover rice if you happen to have it, if not cook, rinse and drain the rice the day before the picnic. Keep the rice in the fridge. Assemble the salad on the morning of the picnic.

fruit skewers

2 large kiwifruit (240g), peeled
2 medium oranges (500g), peeled
¼ seedless watermelon (1.5kg)
½ large pineapple (1kg), peeled
4 strawberries, halved crossways

1   Cut each kiwifruit and orange crossways into four slices. Remove rind from melon, cut fruit into 1.5cm slices. Cut pineapple into 1.5cm slices.
2   Cut 8 x 4.5cm rounds from the kiwifruit and orange slices. Cut 8 x 4.5cm rounds from the watermelon and pineapple slices.
3   Thread alternating slices of fruit onto 8 bamboo skewers, ending with a strawberry.

----

prep time 20 minutes **makes** 8
nutritional count per skewer 0.4g total fat (0g saturated fat); 376kJ (90 cal); 17.4g carbohydrate; 1.9g protein; 4g fibre

Leftover fruit pieces can be used in juices or smoothies. Prepare the skewers the morning of the picnic.

You need 2 medium (240g) carrots to get the amount of grated carrot required for this recipe. Cakes can be made and frosted two days before the picnic; keep covered in the fridge. The cakes can be frozen with or without frosting.

carrot cakes with cream cheese frosting

⅓ cup (80ml) vegetable oil
⅓ cup (75g) caster sugar
1 egg
1 cup firmly packed coarsely grated carrot
¼ cup (30g) finely chopped walnuts
¾ cup (110g) self-raising flour
¼ teaspoon bicarbonate of soda
½ teaspoon mixed spice
cream cheese frosting
20g butter, softened
60g cream cheese, softened
¾ cup (120g) icing sugar

1   Preheat oven to 180°C /160°C fan-forced. Grease 8 holes of 12-hole (½-cup/125ml) oval friand pan.
2   Beat oil, sugar and egg in small bowl with electric mixer until thick and pale. Transfer mixture to large bowl; stir in carrot, nuts and sifted dry ingredients. Spoon mixture evenly into pan holes; bake about 20 minutes.
3   Stand cakes 5 minutes before turning, top-side up, onto wire rack to cool.
4   Make cream cheese frosting. Spread cold cakes with cream cheese frosting. Serve topped with halved walnuts, if you like.

cream cheese frosting Beat butter and cream cheese in small bowl with electric mixer until light and fluffy. Gradually beat in sifted icing sugar.

----

prep & cook time 40 minutes (+ cooling) **makes** 8
nutritional count per cake 17.3g total fat (4.5g saturated fat); 1296kJ (310 cal); 35.7g carbohydrate; 3.7g protein; 1.5g fibre

glossary

APPLES, GOLDEN DELICIOUS a crisp almost citrus-coloured apple with an excellent flavour and good keeping properties. It's probably the best cooking apple around, but you can substitute it with green-skinned granny smiths, another good cooking apple.

BABA GHANOUSH a roasted eggplant (aubergine) dip or spread. It is available from delicatessens and supermarkets.

BACON RASHERS also known as slices of bacon; made from cured, smoked pork side.

BASIL an aromatic herb; there are many types, but the most commonly used is sweet, or common, basil.
pesto a paste made from fresh basil, oil, garlic, pine nuts and parmesan cheese.

BEANS
cannellini a small white bean similar in appearance and flavour to navy, great northern and haricot beans, all of which can be substituted for the other.
green also known as french or string beans; this long thin bean is consumed in its entirety once cooked.
sprouts also known as bean shoots; tender new growths of assorted beans and seeds germinated for consumption. The most readily available are soya beans, mung beans, alfalfa and snow pea sprouts.

BEEF
eye fillet (tenderloin fillet); an expensive, tender and finely textured cut.
rump tender cut taken from the upper part of the hindquarter.

BEETROOT also known as red beets or just beets; firm, round root vegetable.

BICARBONATE OF SODA also known as baking or carb soda; a mild alkali used as a leavening agent in baking.

BREAD
french stick a long, narrow cylindrical loaf having a crisp brown crust and light chewy interior. A standard stick is 5-6cm wide and 3-4cm high, but can be up to a metre in length. It is also known as french bread, french loaf or baguette.
lavash (lavosh) a flat, unleavened bread of Mediterranean origin. Used to wrap fillings, or torn and used for dipping.
melba toasts, mini thinly sliced toasted bread with the crusts removed.
mountain a thin, dry, soft-textured bread used for sandwiches or rolled up and filled with your favourite filling.

par-baked (bake at home rolls) partially-baked bread only needing a few minutes in the oven to give fresh-baked rolls, so you can have fresh, hot bread whenever you want it. Bake only what you need and store the rest.
pitta also known as lebanese bread. This wheat-flour pocket bread is sold in large, flat pieces that separate into two thin rounds. Also available in small thick pieces called pocket pitta.
turkish also known as pide; comes in long (about 45cm) flat loaves as well as individual rounds. Made from wheat flour and sprinkled with sesame seeds or kalonji (black onion seeds).

BURGHUL also known as bulghur wheat; hulled, steamed wheat kernels that, once dried, are crushed into various-sized grains.

BUSH TOMATO RELISH a small, pungent berry from a tomato-related shrub found in central Australia's desert regions. Also called "desert raisin". About 1.5cm long. The relish can be found in speciality food stores and better delicatessens.

BUTTER use salted or unsalted (sweet) butter; 125g equals one stick (4 ounces) of butter.
unsalted butter made without added salt; mainly used in baking. If the recipe calls for unsalted butter, then it should not be substituted.

BUTTERMILK originally the term given to the slightly sour liquid left after butter was churned from cream, today it is commercially made similarly to yogurt. Sold alongside all fresh milk products in supermarkets. Despite the implication of its name, it is low in fat.

CABANOSSI a processed sausage popular in Southern Europe. Made from quality pork and beef and seasoned with selected spices and fresh garlic. Traditionally wood smoked for its unique smoked flavour.

CAPERS the grey-green buds of a warm climate (usually Mediterranean) shrub, sold either dried and salted or pickled in a vinegar brine. Baby capers, those picked early, are small, fuller-flavoured and more expensive than the full-size ones. Rinse well before using.

CAPSICUM also known as bell pepper or pepper. Available in red, green, yellow, orange and purplish-black colours. Discard seeds and membranes before use.

roasted available loose from delis or packed in jars in oil or brine.

CARROTS, BABY also known as dutch carrots. Measuring about 5-8cm long, these small carrots are sold in bunches with the leaves still attached.

CHEESE
bocconcini from the diminutive of boccone meaning 'mouthful', this fresh, walnut-sized, semi-soft, white baby mozzarella spoils rapidly, so must be kept under refrigeration, in brine, for one or two days at most.
cheddar a semi-hard cows-milk cheese. It ranges in colour from white to pale yellow, and has a slightly crumbly texture if properly matured. The flavour becomes sharper, the longer it's aged.
cream commonly known as Philly or Philadelphia; a soft cows-milk cheese. Also available as spreadable light cream cheese, which is a blend of cottage and cream cheeses.
fetta a crumbly goat- or sheep-milk cheese with a sharp salty taste.
goat made from goats milk; has an earthy, strong taste; available in soft and firm textures, in various shapes and sizes, sometimes rolled in ash or herbs.
haloumi a firm, cream-coloured sheep-milk cheese matured in brine; somewhat like a minty, salty fetta in flavour, haloumi can be grilled or fried, briefly, without breaking down. Should be eaten while still warm as it becomes tough and rubbery on cooling.
parmesan also known as parmigiano; a hard, grainy, cows-milk cheese. The curd is salted in brine for a month before being aged for up to two years in humid conditions.
ricotta the name for this soft, white, cows-milk cheese roughly translates as 'cooked again'. It's made from whey, a by-product of other cheese-making. Is a sweet, moist cheese with a slightly grainy texture.
manchego an aged, semi-firm, intensely flavoured Spanish cheese made from sheep milk. Available from specialty cheese stores; substitute haloumi or fetta if not readily available.
roquefort a firm, blue-veined cheese with a rich and piquant taste.

CHICKEN DRUMETTES small fleshy part of the wing between the shoulder and elbow, trimmed to resemble a drumstick. Also called wingettes.

CHICKPEAS also called garbanzos, channa or hummus; round, sandy-coloured legume.

CHILLI available in many different types and sizes; generally the smaller the chilli, the hotter it is. Use rubber gloves when seeding and chopping fresh chillies as they can burn your skin. Removing seeds and membranes lessens the heat level.

CHIPOLATA also known as 'little fingers'; highly spiced, coarsely-textured sausage up to 7cm in length. Traditionally made with pork, but beef may also be used.

CHOCOLATE
dark cooking also known as compounded chocolate; good for cooking as it sets at room temperature. Made with vegetable fat instead of cocoa butter.
dark eating also known as semi-sweet or luxury chocolate; made of a high percentage of cocoa liquor and cocoa butter, and a little added sugar.
Melts discs of dark compound chocolate ideal for melting and moulding.
white contains no cocoa solids but derives its sweet flavour from cocoa butter. Very sensitive to heat, so watch carefully when melting.

CHORIZO a sausage of Spanish origin; made of coarsely ground pork and highly seasoned with garlic and chillies.

COCOA POWDER also known as cocoa; dried, unsweetened, roasted then ground cocoa beans (cacao seeds).

COCONUT
desiccated unsweetened, concentrated, dried, finely shredded coconut.
milk the second pressing (less rich) from grated mature coconut flesh; available in cans and cartons.
shredded long thin strips of dried coconut (longer, thicker and more course than desiccated coconut).

COPPA is a salted and dried sausage made from the neck or shoulder of pork. It is deep red in colour and can be found in both mild and spicy versions.

CORIANDER also known as pak chee, cilantro or chinese parsley; bright-green leafy herb with a pungent flavour. Both the stems and roots of coriander are used in Thai cooking; wash well before using. Also available ground or as seeds; these should not be substituted for fresh coriander, however, as the tastes are completely different.

CORNFLOUR also known as cornstarch; used as a thickening agent. Available as 100% maize (corn) and wheaten cornflour.

CORNICHONS French for gherkin, a very small variety of cucumber.

COUSCOUS a fine, grain-like cereal product made from semolina. A semolina flour and water dough is sieved then dehydrated to produce minuscule even sized pellets of couscous; it is rehydrated by steaming, or with the addition of a warm liquid, and swells to three or four times its original size.

CREAM we used fresh cream, also known as pure cream and pouring cream, unless otherwise stated.
double has a 60-66% fat content.
sour a thick, commercially cultured soured cream.
thickened a whipping cream containing a thickener.

CUCUMBER, LEBANESE short, slender and thin-skinned. Probably the most popular variety because of its tender, edible skin, tiny, yielding seeds, and sweet, fresh and flavoursome taste.

CUMIN also known as zeera or comino.

DUCK, CHINESE BARBECUED traditionally cooked in special ovens, this duck has a sweet-sticky coating made from soy sauce, sherry, five-spice and hoisin sauce. It is available from Asian food stores.

EGGPLANT purple-skinned vegetable also known as aubergine. Also available char-grilled, packed in oil, in jars.

FENNEL also known as finocchio or anise; a white to very pale green-white, firm, crisp, roundish vegetable about 8-12cm in diameter. The bulb has a slightly sweet, anise flavour but the leaves have a much stronger taste. Also the name given to dried seeds having a licorice flavour.

FLOUR
flour, plain an all-purpose flour made from wheat.
self-raising plain flour sifted with baking powder in the proportion of 1 cup flour to 2 teaspoons baking powder.

GELATINE a thickening agent. We used powdered gelatine. It is also available in sheet form, known as leaf gelatine.

GRISSINI pencil-sized sticks of crispy, dry bread.

HAZELNUTS also known as filberts.

To remove skin the brown inedible skin of this plump, grape-sized, rich, sweet nut is removed by rubbing heated nuts together vigorously in a tea towel.
meal also known as ground hazelnuts.

HORSERADISH CREAM a commercially prepared creamy paste made of grated horseradish, vinegar, oil and sugar.

KAFFIR LIME LEAVES also known as bai magrood; look like two glossy dark green leaves joined end to end, forming a rounded hourglass shape. A strip of fresh lime peel may be substituted for each kaffir lime leaf.

LETTUCE
butter small with round, loosely formed heads having soft, buttery-textured leaves ranging from pale green on the outer leaves to pale yellow-green on the inner leaves. Has a sweet flavour.
cos also known as romaine lettuce.
endive, baby a leafy green lettuce with crisp leaves and a pale heart. Has a slightly bitter flavour.
witlof cigar-shaped lettuce with tightly packed heads with pale, yellow-green tips. Has a delicately bitter flavour. May be cooked or eaten raw.

LIQUEUR use your own favourite brand, if you like.
coconut-flavoured we use Malibu.
coffee-flavoured we use Kahlúa.
orange-flavoured we use Grand Marnier.

MAYONNAISE we prefer to use whole egg mayonnaise in our recipes.

MINCE also known as ground meat.

MIRIN is a Japanese champagne-coloured cooking wine made of glutinous rice and alcohol and used expressly for cooking. Should not be confused with sake.

MIXED SPICE a blend of ground spices usually consisting of cinnamon, allspice and nutmeg.

MORELLO CHERRIES a dark sour cherry used in both sweet and savoury dishes. Available from most supermarkets.

MUSHROOMS
flat large, flat mushrooms with a rich earthy flavour, ideal for filling and barbecuing. They are sometimes misnamed field mushrooms, which are wild mushrooms.
swiss brown also known as cremini or roman, light to dark brown mushrooms with a full-bodied flavour.

MUSTARD

dijon a pale brown, distinctively flavoured, fairly mild french mustard.

powder finely ground white (yellow) mustard seeds.

wholegrain also known as seeded. A French-style coarse-grain mustard made from crushed mustard seeds and dijon-style french mustard.

NOODLES, GREEN TEA soba noodles made of buckwheat and wheat flour with the added ingredient of fresh green tea leaves. In Japan they are considered a delicacy, and are only consumed on very special occasions.

ONIONS

green also known as scallion or, incorrectly, shallot; an immature onion picked before the bulb has formed, having a long, bright-green edible stalk.

red also known as spanish, red spanish or bermuda onion; a sweet-flavoured, large, purple-red onion.

shallot also called french shallots, golden shallots or eschalots; small, brown-skinned, elongated members of the onion family. Grows in tight clusters similar to garlic.

spring onions with small white bulbs and long, narrow green leaves.

PAPRIKA a ground dried sweet red capsicum (bell pepper); there are many types available, including sweet, hot, mild and smoked. Available from supermarkets, delicatessens and speciality food stores.

PARSLEY, FLAT-LEAF a flat-leaf variety of parsley also known as continental or italian parsley.

PEKING DUCK PANCAKES small, round crêpes or pancakes made with plain flour; can be purchased commercially from Asian food stores. To prepare pancakes, place in a steamer set over a large pan of simmering water and steam about 5 minutes or until warm and pliable.

PENNE PASTA translated literally as 'quills'; ridged pasta cut into short lengths on the diagonal. Great with chunky sauces.

PISTACHIOS pale green, delicately flavoured nut inside hard off-white shells. To peel, soak shelled nuts in boiling water for about 5 minutes; drain, then pat dry with absorbent paper. Rub skins with cloth to peel.

PIZZA BASES pre-packaged for home-made pizzas. They come in a variety of sizes (snack or family) and thicknesses (thin and crispy or thick). Available with or without sauce.

POTATOES, KIPFLER small, finger-shaped, knobby potato with a nutty flavour.

PRAWNS also known as shrimp.

PRESERVED LEMON RIND a North African specialty; lemons are quartered and preserved in salt and lemon juice. To use, remove and discard pulp, squeeze juice from rind then rinse rind well and slice thinly. Sold in jars or singly by delicatessens; once opened, store under refrigeration.

PROSCIUTTO a kind of unsmoked Italian ham; salted, air-cured and aged.

QUAILS small, delicately flavoured, domestically grown game birds ranging in weight from 250g to 300g; also known as partridge.

ROCKET also known as arugula, rugula and rucola; a peppery-tasting green leaf. Baby rocket leaves (wild rocket) are both smaller and less peppery.

SAUCES

fish also called nam pla or nuoc nam; made from pulverised salted fermented fish, most often anchovies. Has a pungent smell and strong taste, so use sparingly.

hoisin a thick, sweet and spicy chinese paste made from salted fermented soya beans, onions and garlic; used as a marinade or baste.

sweet chilli a comparatively mild, Thai-style sauce made from red chillies, sugar, garlic and vinegar.

Tabasco brand name of an extremely fiery sauce made from vinegar, thai red chillies and salt.

worcestershire a dark coloured condiment made from garlic, soy sauce, tamarind, onions, molasses, anchovies, vinegar, lime and seasonings. Available from most supermarkets.

SNOW PEAS also called mange tout ('eat all'). Tendrils, the growing shoots of the plant, are sold by greengrocers, while the sprouts are tender new growths of snow peas.

SPINACH also known as english spinach and, incorrectly, silver beet.

SUGAR

brown an extremely soft, finely granulated sugar retaining molasses for its characteristic colour and flavour.

caster also known as superfine or finely granulated table sugar.

icing also known as confectioners' sugar or powdered sugar; granulated sugar crushed together with a small amount of cornflour added.

white a coarse, granulated table sugar, also known as crystal sugar.

SUGAR SNAP PEAS also known as honey snap peas; a fresh small pea that can be eaten whole, pod and all, similarly to snow peas.

SUMAC a purple-red, astringent spice ground from berries growing on shrubs that flourish around the Mediterranean; adds a tart, lemony flavour to recipes.

TURMERIC, GROUND related to galangal and ginger; imparts a golden colour to dishes of which it's a part.

VANILLA

bean dried long, thin pod from a tropical golden orchid; the minuscule black seeds inside the bean are used to impart a luscious vanilla flavour in baking and desserts.

extract made by pulping chopped vanilla beans with a mixture of alcohol and water. This gives a very strong solution, and only a couple of drops are needed to flavour most dishes.

VINEGAR

red wine based on fermented red wine.

rice wine made from rice wine lees (sediment), salt and alcohol.

sherry made from a blend of wines and left in wood vats to mature where they develop a rich mellow flavour.

white wine made from white wine.

WATERCRESS also known as winter rocket; one of the cress family, a large group of peppery greens. Highly perishable, so must be used as soon as possible after purchase.

YOGURT we used plain, unflavoured yogurt, unless otherwise specified.

ZA'ATAR is a blend of whole roasted sesame seeds, sumac and crushed dried herbs such as wild marjoram and thyme; its content is largely determined by the individual maker. Used to flavour many Middle-Eastern dishes. It is available from delicatessens and specialty food stores or you can make your own.

ZUCCHINI also known as courgette; small, pale- or dark-green, yellow or white vegetable belonging to the squash family.

conversion chart

MEASURES

One Australian metric measuring cup holds approximately 250ml; one Australian metric tablespoon holds 20ml; one Australian metric teaspoon holds 5ml.

The difference between one country's measuring cups and another's is within a two- or three-teaspoon variance, and will not affect your cooking results. North America, New Zealand and the United Kingdom use a 15ml tablespoon.

All cup and spoon measurements are level. The most accurate way of measuring dry ingredients is to weigh them. When measuring liquids, use a clear glass or plastic jug with the metric markings.

We use large eggs with an average weight of 60g.

DRY MEASURES

METRIC	IMPERIAL
15g	½oz
30g	1oz
60g	2oz
90g	3oz
125g	4oz (¼lb)
155g	5oz
185g	6oz
220g	7oz
250g	8oz (½lb)
280g	9oz
315g	10oz
345g	11oz
375g	12oz (¾lb)
410g	13oz
440g	14oz
470g	15oz
500g	16oz (1lb)
750g	24oz (1½lb)
1kg	32oz (2lb)

LIQUID MEASURES

METRIC	IMPERIAL
30ml	1 fluid oz
60ml	2 fluid oz
100ml	3 fluid oz
125ml	4 fluid oz
150ml	5 fluid oz (¼ pint/1 gill)
190ml	6 fluid oz
250ml	8 fluid oz
300ml	10 fluid oz (½ pint)
500ml	16 fluid oz
600ml	20 fluid oz (1 pint)
1000ml (1 litre)	1¾ pints

LENGTH MEASURES

METRIC	IMPERIAL
3mm	⅛in
6mm	¼in
1cm	½in
2cm	¾in
2.5cm	1in
5cm	2in
6cm	2½in
8cm	3in
10cm	4in
13cm	5in
15cm	6in
18cm	7in
20cm	8in
23cm	9in
25cm	10in
28cm	11in
30cm	12in (1ft)

OVEN TEMPERATURES

These oven temperatures are only a guide for conventional ovens. For fan-forced ovens, check the manufacturer's manual.

	°C (CELSIUS)	°F (FAHRENHEIT)	GAS MARK
Very slow	120	250	½
Slow	150	275-300	1-2
Moderately slow	160	325	3
Moderate	180	350-375	4-5
Moderately hot	200	400	6
Hot	220	425-450	7-8
Very hot	240	475	9

index

ACP Books

General manager Christine Whiston
Editor-in-chief Susan Tomnay
Creative director & designer Hieu Chi Nguyen
Art director Hannah Blackmore
Senior editor Wendy Bryant
Food director Pamela Clark
Nutritional information Nicole Jennings
Recipe development Kate Nichols
Sales & rights director Brian Cearnes
Marketing manager Bridget Cody
Senior business analyst Rebecca Varela
Circulation manager Jama Mclean
Operations manager David Scotto
Production manager Victoria Jefferys

ACP Books are published by ACP Magazines a division of PBL Media Pty Limited
PBL Media, Chief Executive Officer Ian Law
Publishing & sales director, Women's lifestyle Lynette Phillips
General manager, Editorial projects, Women's lifestyle Deborah Thomas
Editor at Large, Women's lifestyle Pat Ingram
Marketing director, Women's lifestyle Matthew Dominello
Commercial manager, Women's lifestyle Seymour Cohen
Research director, Women's lifestyle Justin Stone

Produced by ACP Books, Sydney.

Published by ACP Books, a division of ACP Magazines Ltd, 54 Park St, Sydney; GPO Box 4088, Sydney, NSW 2001.
phone (02) 9282 8618; fax (02) 9267 9438. acpbooks@acpmagazines.com.au; www.acpbooks.com.au

Printed by Toppan Printing Co, China.

Australia Distributed by Network Services, phone +61 2 9282 8777; fax +61 2 9264 3278;
networkweb@networkservicescompany.com.au
United Kingdom Distributed by Australian Consolidated Press (UK), phone (01604) 642 200;
fax (01604) 642 300; books@acpuk.com
New Zealand Distributed by Netlink Distribution Company, phone (9) 366
South Africa Distributed by PSD Promotions, phone (27 11) 3
fax (27 11) 392 6079/80; orders@psdprom.co.za
Canada Distributed by Publishers Group Canada
phone (800) 663 5714; fax (800) 565 3770; service@rainc

Title: Perfect picnics / food director Pamela Clark.
ISBN: 978 1 86396 866 9 (pbk.)
Notes: Includes index.
Subjects: Picnicking.
Other Authors/Contributors: Clark, Pamela.
Also Titled: Australian women's weekly.
Dewey Number: 641.578
© ACP Magazines Ltd 2009
ABN 18 053 273 546
This publication is copyright. No part of it may be reproduced or transm
without the written permission of the publishers.

Photographer Andre Martin **Stylist** Vicki Liley **Food preparation**

The publishers would like to thank the following for props used in
Honey Bee Homewares, Ici et la, Michael's shoppe

Send recipe enquiries to:
recipeenquiries@acpmagazines.com.au